Becoming A Truck Driver: The Raw Truth About Truck Driving

By Brett Aquila

Raw Truth – The REAL Driver Experience

Ok, we'll be covering some of the general information you wanted to know about the types of jobs available in the industry, but for now, let's get down to the really good stuff you'll need to know...the Raw Truth. There are a number of different entities you will have to deal with and understand as a driver including your own company, the shippers and receivers, and the DOT. Now I'm telling you, you've come to the right place.

No matter which of these entities you talk with you're going to get nothing but propaganda and/or recruiting. You need The Truth about these entities...what are their agendas, what are they really offering me, how will I be treated once I get hired, when can I expect for home time, etc. I'm going to cover all of that and a whole lot more.

I'm also going to provide you with tons of hints, tips, tricks, and my own personal stories about dealing with each entity and how to make the system work for you. Once you understand these entities and the systems they use you will be in a much better position to make things work in your favor instead of beating your head against the wall by saying the wrong things to the wrong people or having false expectations.

Ok, let's get started with your journey by telling you about mine!

The Journey Begins

So at this point you're wondering what life will be like if you do decide to become a driver.

The path most new drivers will take will be to attend a school, get hired by a company, go on the road for a few weeks with a trainer, and then get your own truck and you're off! So let's start at the beginning with the schooling. This is my story.

How It All Started

I was 21 years old and working at a warehouse outside of Atlanta, GA. I'm originally from Buffalo, NY where I now reside 14 years later. But when we were 19, a couple of buddies of mine and I jumped in an old van and drove from Buffalo, NY to Atlanta, GA on a wing and a prayer. We were all about the adventure. Actually, I was all about the adventure and LOVED dragging others into my adventures with me so off we went!

After a couple of really fun years my one buddy and I found ourselves working for $5.50 an hour in a warehouse. We worked a ton of hours and enjoyed it. The people we worked with were great and we partied a lot! We damn sure weren't getting rich, but we were getting by.

One day we got to work and saw a large six wheel rental truck sitting in the parking lot. I asked the boss what was up. He said we had some pallets we had to run into downtown Atlanta (about 10 or 15 miles maybe) and pick up some others and bring em back.

Well, I had never even seen the inside of one of those trucks, let alone drive one. I knew they were automatics and figured I could drive it easy enough. I eagerly volunteered for the task. My boss asked with a skeptical look, "have you ever driven a truck like that before?" and like any responsible adult looking for an opportunity to try something new I lied my brains out!!!!!

I said' "Oh yeah! My aunt moved twice and my grandma moved once and all three times we needed a truck that size and I drove it." He continued with that skeptical look and said he'd talk to the other boss and let me know.

Well, I bugged him repeatedly for the next hour or two and to my absolute delight they said I could do it! I was freakin! This was gonna be a blast! At least I had hoped so. Hell, I had never done it before but what the hell... it'll be fun I'm sure! So we loaded up the truck and off I went.

It handled like a big pickup truck. Nothing to it. So I cruised down into the city, found my destination, and made the delivery. Well, before they could reload me it was their lunchtime. So I wandered the city for about 45 minutes, came back, they reloaded me, and off I went back to the warehouse.

By the time I got back there it was almost time to go home for the day. I laughed about it and told my buddy, "Wow, I really got away with one. I didn't even have to do any work today. All I had to do was drive!", and IMMEDIATELY the light turned on in my head. What about becoming a truck driver????

I had no experience with it and knew nothing about it. I also didn't know any truck drivers so I went home that day and called the only trucking company I knew the name of off the top of my head. I asked, "how much do you make your first year as a driver?", and they said about $35,000. THIRTY FIVE THOUSAND DOLLARS! MY GOD I'D BE RICH AND WOULDN'T HAVE TO WORK! (I was young and getting by on about one third of that at the time remember... those were good times.

In fact we were so happy when we were told we'd be making $5.50 an hour that we did a ridiculous dance the moment the boss left.... a dance that came to be know from then on as the 550 dance!).

So I immediately called a private trucking school and made an appointment. My ma said she would pay for the schooling for me (I gave her a combination of a good sales pitch and guilt) and within a month I was in school... the start of my odyssey.

Now why did I pick a private school? Well, that was kinda lucky really. There are private schools and then there are trucking companies that have their own schools. I didn't even know that there were trucking companies that had their own schools!

So I found a private one in the area and looked into their reputation. They seemed to be the best around...and they were. So I did enough research to pick a good private school, but you may want to attend school at a trucking company. Let's briefly cover the two types to give you an idea of your options.

Types Of Schools

Generally speaking there are a couple different types of schools you can attend. Honestly this isn't necessarily that critical of a decision. I have known tons of people that have gone through one type or the other and both seem to do just fine. There are a couple things you should know though.

Private Schools

Private schools are not associated with any particular trucking company. They are run independently so students upon graduation can choose to go anywhere they would like. The schools range in price generally from $2000-$5000 and can take anywhere from 3 weeks to 8 weeks to complete for your Class A license. It would take less time and money if you only wanted a Class B but I strongly suggest you avoid going that route. You are not only embarking on a new job, it's a new career.

By only getting your Class B license you are severely limiting yourself not only with regard to the number of jobs available to you but the amount of money you can make. It only costs a little more money and takes a little bit more time to get your Class A and believe me you won't regret it. Almost anyone I have ever talked to with a Class B had plans for getting their Class A, but I've never once talked to anyone that wished they had only gotten their Class B. Nobody. Go for your Class A.

Many of the better private schools will have a wide range of training including several weeks of practice at backing up the truck, classroom coverage of everything from log books to maps and routing to air brakes and vehicle inspection. They will also have several weeks of training out on the local roadways.

Make sure they will give you the necessary training to get ALL of your endorsements including hazmat, tankers, doubles and triples, and people (buses). Make sure you get ALL of these. It only requires a very short written test and can also severely limit your job opportunities if you leave them out.

Be sure to ask the school what their policy is if you don't pass the driving portion of the test for your CDL the first time. A reputable school will continue to work with you for a short period of time to allow you the extra practice you need. They can't guarantee you'll pass it, but they will continue to help you for some time.

Also, most good schools have a job placement program. There is a HUGE demand for drivers nationwide and their job placement department will have a long list of companies willing to hire you the day you graduate. You can tell them the type of job you are looking for and they will have several choices for you. Believe me, getting a job coming out of school is very, very easy. But getting the right job for you at the right company will be much more likely if you have some experienced help with good contacts.

Many schools will also offer financial aid. The money you are required to put up front is sometimes a big limiting factor on what type of school you can attend. Offering financial aid can open up your opportunities. Find out how long it will be before you are required to begin making payments after graduation. Most schools will allow you 3-6 months before you start making payments.

The advantage to attending a private school is that the training is general for the industry, not specific to one company. Therefore it will apply no matter where you choose to work and will not be geared toward any one company's particular equipment or agenda.

The disadvantage is that it may cost you more money up front if you aren't eligible for financial aid.

Trucking Company School

Some trucking companies offer their own schools. This can also be a good option but be aware of a couple differences.

For starters, a company is going to train you according to what THEY want out of you. They have a certain set of equipment, a certain set of rules, and sometimes a certain type of freight. For instance, many of the bigger companies now have fleets of fully automatic trucks. You won't learn how to manually shift a truck which will severely limit your options if you decide to go elsewhere.

Secondly a trucking company will make a trade-off with you. They will often require little or no money up front but instead will allow you to pay back the money by paying you a little bit less and requiring you to remain with them for a certain period of time, usually one year. This is sometimes a necessary trade off if you can't afford the up front money or qualify for financial aid at a private school.

If you do decide to go this route find out what the company's policy is on paying them back if you don't fulfill your obligation to them. Generally they will prorate the amount you owe them based on how long you worked there.

An example of a company specific policy could be mountain braking. There are several different schools of thought on proper braking techniques for going down a mountain. If a company's safety department is convinced that one particular way is the best way then they may not even cover any other theories, or possibly even try to convince you that any other way will be disastrous.

As you know there are usually a number of different ways to accomplish something and since you will be the one whose life is on the line, wouldn't you like to know all of the options so you can use your own judgment and have a more thorough understanding of the topic?

Also, every company has different policies when it comes to your logbook. Some have much tighter regulations than others. Whatever their policy is will be the only way they will teach it. Often times a company will require things above and beyond the federal DOT guidelines. These requirements may be a hindrance at a company with more lenient policies. Be aware of this type of teaching.

Personally I haven't come across anybody who regretted their schooling decision. The major reason for this is that you will really only learn about 5% of what you will

REALLY need to know in school. The rest you will learn from experience. Once you get your license and get one year of safe driving experience under your belt the sky is the limit. Pretty much any company in the country will hire you with those simple credentials.

Let The Schooling Begin

So I'd chosen my school, ma paid for it, and I showed up for the first day. Welcome. Smiling faces, hand shakes, and piles and piles of paperwork on each desk. No party hats (they really should have party hats) but, oh well, what do they know?

The schooling began with nothing but classroom study for the first week or two. If you decide to attend school at a trucking company....let the propaganda begin! They won't waste any chance at promoting themselves, believe me. They will also make you feel like it is your privilege to be working for them. Get used to that. Now here's your first piece of raw truth about the industry... companies are completely and totally desperate for drivers. I mean DESPERATE!

Were you ever offered a $2000 bonus just to come work for a company? Did you ever have a company offer to pay for all of your schooling if you will come work for them when you graduate? Why would someone offer such an insane amount of money just for you to come work there? They don't even know you! They have no idea what you're capable of! You don't even have any experience! They don't really care.

These bonuses are common at the larger companies. Sure they HOPE you're gonna be an awesome driver, but more than anything they just desperately need your butt in one of their trucks. Period.

Well, turnover is a huge problem in the trucking industry. A driver with a clean record, even a driver straight out of school, can land literally hundreds or even thousands of jobs at any time and everybody knows that, drivers and companies alike. So in order to put themselves in a position of authority, which is a falsity, they may try to keep you on pins and needles by implying that your job is always on the line. One false move and you could be fired.

This is one of the HUGE mistakes that companies make.... its simply not true.

All that they really accomplish by trying to scare you is filling you with a lack of trust and loyalty towards them. Most large companies are full of drivers that have hit bridges, rolled trucks, been late for deliveries, and on and on. Does this mean you won't ever get fired? Certainly not. I've been fired a few times by idiots I've never met on some committee making decisions based on little or no real facts or understanding about me or my situation.

But getting another job, as long as you've never had a DUI or killed somebody, is really easy...so don't let them snow you into thinking your career is always on the line... it's a bluff. Lose your job and you can have ten new ones tomorrow. Simple as that. Ok now back to the classroom.

Now if you've chosen a private school, which is the road I chose, you won't have nearly the bologna to deal with. The schools are independent of all trucking companies and they've already gotten your money so there's no reason to push any sort of self serving agenda. They have no reason to BS you.

What they DO need to do is give you the very best experience they can while you attend their school and give you the best chance they can give you at being successful once you've graduated. Their entire future is based upon their reputation. Word of mouth from former students and recommendations from the trucking companies they send students to are the key to their future survival.

If you don't like your experience and the students coming out of the school aren't satisfactory to the companies they go to work for then the school is going to die a long, slow death. Nobody will want to attend. So they will get straight to work filling you with information.... and tons of it.

No matter which type of school you decide upon the first week or two will be similar... classwork. Videos, slide shows, workbooks, charts, and a few written tests sprinkled in here and there. To be honest the work is really pretty easy. But be aware... they are going to completely and totally overwhelm you with the sheer quantity of information... and they know it.

Being a truck driver, especially over the road or regional, requires far more knowledge than most people outside the industry would ever begin to imagine. Every state has its own set of rules, regulations, and procedures. Go from New York to Los Angeles and you will cross through about a dozen states.

That's a dozen different sets of rules. Some rules will be common to each state but each state will have some unique rules you must be familiar with. Now don't let this scare you... everybody has learned to deal with it and you will too.

The learning curve is really steep in the beginning. The schools have to give you all the information they can because if you get out there and make a mistake your company may call the school and say,"didn't you teach this?" The school can usually say they gave you the information but you must not have used it. That's the schools job... to give you the information. It's your job to learn it and use it.

Again, please don't let this scare you. It's intimidating at first, but you'll learn as you go. Everybody goes through this steep learning curve in the beginning and you will too.

So you'll spend a week or so in the classroom and generally the next couple of weeks will be a combination of classroom time and learning to back up the truck through a variety of different obstacles. Now if you're like me you may have never even been in a big rig until now... and let me tell ya it's really, really fun.. especially at a private school. Private schools will take their time and won't pressure you.

Remember, they want you to enjoy your learning experience so you will recommend their school to others. Trucking companies are hit and miss... some of them may push you and pressure you to keep their agenda alive... it's YOUR privilege to be working there so you BETTER perform.

Now not all of them will treat you this way. A lot it will depend on the individual instructors. But a lot of the instructors at the trucking companies have worked for these companies for many, many years and so feel like they're the king and you better revere them. It's just like anything else.... some people let a tiny bit of authority and experience go straight to their heads. Here's a story for you....

After 9 years in the industry and 2 1/2 years at one particular trucking company I decided to return to that company after I had quit to try other things about 6 months prior.

By law the company has to give all new hires a "road test" which usually just entails about a 10 minute drive down the road and back. Well, anybody with 6 months experience can take an 8 hour class to be eligible to give road tests at this particular company and most large companies aren't much different.

So I meet the "road test dude" and we hop in the truck. He had no idea the level of experience I had. I already had 250,000 safe miles of driving in all 48 states and Canada just with this company alone! So I'm just relaxed and we're talking as I pull out of the parking lot and up a long steep hill to a stop sign. I've never driven this particular truck and every truck has a slightly different feel to the clutch. They are adjusted differently and require different amounts of movement and pressure depending upon a number of factors.

So I stop at the sign, traffic clears, and I get ready to roll. The hill is steep and I didn't quite let the clutch out the perfect amount before getting off the brake and the truck eased back about 6 inches before the clutch grabbed and the truck rolled forward. The distance it rolled and the time period it happened in was so small that by the time he screamed," WE'RE ROLLING BACKWARDS!!!" we were already rolling forward.

It was a massive overreaction on his part and was quite comical to me. I laughed and said, "Take it easy man, I know. Don't freak", and I kept chuckling. He yells," YOU KNOW I CAN FAIL YOU FOR THAT!" and I smiled and said,"Man, how long have you been driving and how long have you been at this company?" He said three years driving, six months with the company.

I said, "Man, I've been driving for a total of nine years with nearly one million safe miles (this is not an exaggeration) and 2 ½ years with 250,000 safe miles at this company alone. Now we can turn around and go back and you can tell them I've failed your driving test and that I'm not qualified to drive for this company in your opinion or we can kick back, relax and enjoy the rest of this ride." It turned out to be quite a kicked-back, relaxed, and enjoyable ride.

So no matter where you go you will get some of these authoritarian types but don't let em get to ya. They're idiots. The instructors who really care about teaching you all that they can will be very patient and understanding. Nobody is born with the ability to drive a big rig. We all had to learn from scratch. The good instructors haven't forgotten that.

Ok so you've spent a couple weeks in the classroom and backing up the truck. Now the time usually switches to a mix of backing up and actual driving out on the road. Little or no classwork will be required anymore. The nice thing about getting your CDL is that the schools pretty much already know exactly what the written and driving tests will involve. Both the private and trucking company schools have one goal – getting you to pass that test. They both have a HUGE interest at stake. The more students that pass the test the more it will help them... so they are genuinely interested in giving you what you need to get your license.

As you would expect the road portion will generally be in a safe area. They don't want too much pressure on you as a student and they don't want to risk an accident. So don't panic... the road portion of the training is also tons of fun. Believe me, after backing up in a parking lot for weeks you will be very, very eager to get on the road and actually drive FORWARD! You surely will never forget the first time you ever get to do it for real... I certainly haven't.

There wasn't anything eventful about my first time. I got it rolling, got onto the roadway, started going through the gears, and cruised around for about 10 minutes on an open highway. When my turn was up (they bring 3 or 4 students in each truck at a time and take turns) I pulled to the side, got out, and looked back at the truck. I couldn't BELIEVE I had just driven a building on wheels!!! Actually, it was pretty easy!!! I was soooo excited.... we all were.

After weeks of work and often times months of planning it was finally coming together. We finally did it for real and realized that we were really on our way to becoming real truck drivers! A new, exciting, and much higher paying career for almost all of us. Wow, what a feeling!

I remember the hotel I stayed at was right next to the interstate. The school I attended was 7 weeks long. Every night I used to walk across the bridge over the interstate to go get something to eat. I would stop on that bridge and watch the trucks pass underneath and just dream about my chance to do it someday soon.

They were REAL truck drivers and they were REALLY traveling to far away places, making great money! I would watch 'em pass into the distance wondering where they came from, where they were heading to, and most of all what it would feel like when I was doing it for real.

I knew someday soon a class would come into that same school behind me and those students would be dreaming of their day as they watched me fade away into distance. Those were really, really good times. And I can tell ya it turned out to be everything I'd ever hoped it would be and so much more! I really did pass under that same bridge dozens and dozens of times over the years.

Every time I did I would look at that hotel and wave to the school and smile. I never forget how excited I was back then and I was always so thankful for having the career I have. It's been great. We'll get to a lot more stories soon. But for now, on with the schooling.

So the time to start taking the CDL tests is drawing near. You would think it would be a nervous time for all of us but it really wasn't. The school I went to was the best and we all felt quite comfortable that we were very well prepared. Most of the written test questions we had been practicing for weeks would be word for word the same as on the actual test. And the driving portion of the test was EXACTLY the same thing as we had been practicing.

There are three parts to the test... the written, the backing up, and the road test. The written you can do in your sleep. The backing had a couple challenging parts but after six straight weeks of practicing we all knew we had it down. The road portion was also easy... easier than the backing portion I would say.

In a class of 27 people we all passed and got our CDL. All of us. So don't let any insecurities you may have toward passing the test play a factor in your decision to go for your CDL. With a little bit of effort almost anybody can do it. There are millions and millions of truck drivers in this country that have done it and surely if they were all capable of it so are you.

What is the chance that millions of people can do something that's relatively simple but you cant? I can say with near certainty – none. Don't let passing these tests concern you... they're easy. Forget about it!

So we passed our tests, we had our CDL, and on came graduation day. Now I was always very competitive and wanted to finish first in my class. With a lot hard work I did it by the narrowest of margins. Did it matter? Well, yes and no. I could have gotten the same job I wound up getting directly out of school even if my grades weren't as good as they were, but it wouldn't have been as easy as it was.

We were eating pizza and drinking our sodas when we noticed a big rig pull into the parking lot. Nice truck! Well a guy gets out, shakes hands with several of the school's instructors, and grabs a soda. A few minutes later I hear him ask, “so, who were the top three guys?” The instructor pointed us out and the guy came over and introduced himself.

He said if we weren't too busy he'd like us to follow him about a mile up the road to his company's terminal so we could fill out the paperwork, go get our physicals, and get started. Can you believe it? We were hired on the spot! I hadn't even finished my pizza yet!

So we followed him there, filled out the paperwork, went to get our physical, and within about 3 hours of finishing our pizza we were officially the three newest employees of the company! I think I had pizza sauce on my shirt! Didn't matter, we were in! Wow, what a day!

So you're wondering if that's how it really went. Am I exaggerating? Do I have a secret agenda? I'm telling ya.. that's EXACTLY how it really went. Have times changed? Yap – FOR THE BETTER! Believe it or not, back then companies had higher hiring standards than they do now. Now wait..they hired me on the spot on graduation day... how could standards get LOWER?

Well, back then most companies required you to be 23 or 25 years of age, never failed a drug test, never had a DUI, and many companies wanted a clean or fairly clean driving record. Nowadays, most companies require you to be 21 years of age, haven't failed a drug test in the past two years, and haven't had a DUI in the past seven years.

Yes, believe it or not they are so desperate for drivers that they will even consider you even after you've failed a drug test or had a DUI in your past. Not all companies of course, but some.

As far as your driving record goes, most will accept minor accidents and tickets, even in a truck, as long as you haven't had any recent charges of reckless driving or DUI. Also they may not accept you if you've been found liable in an accident involving serious injuries or death... but this varies from company to company.

If you have a questionable driving or criminal record simply get these records from your local police and driving agencies and present them to a few large trucking companies to see what they say. This will give you a good idea of how difficult getting hired may or may not be.

So I made it through the schooling, got my CDL, and was hired by my first company. Now the fun part really begins... out on the road for real. So do they just throw you in a truck and say, “Good luck, don't crash”? Nope, you've got a little bit of help in between... your trainer.

But before we get to that, I'd like to take a little bit of time to talk about some important factors in deciding what company you should start your career with. I started out with a large company driving over the road and pulling a dry van so first I'm going to explain what you can expect from an over the road job.

After that I'll cover what pulling a dry van is all about and then we'll cover some tips on choosing your first company. I'll cover the other types of trucks along with regional and local jobs later on as I get to those parts of my career.

Types Of Jobs

There are three major categories of driving jobs: over the road (long distance), regional, and local. Each has some similarities, but there are several MAJOR differences that will be key in choosing which is right for you. Let's start with over the road.

Over The Road

Over the road driving usually entails staying out on the road for at least three weeks at a time. Let me say this right off...if you have a family, and you would like to KEEP that family....stay away from this option. It's a family killer. I've seen it a million times. If you're single, don't have any children, and like the idea of traveling the country and actually living a nomadic lifestyle...this is for you.

When I started driving I was 21 years old. I had never been married, had no children, and hadn't traveled much. The idea of living on the road and seeing the entire country coast to coast sounded awesome! So off I went. It was one of the best decisions of my life.

Over the road is much more than just a job...it is a lifestyle. Traveling the country, living in the truck, and never knowing where the next load might take you becomes your life. Yes, you get to go home every few weeks, but you'll find that you are no longer part of the everyday lives of your family and friends, so you will be treated more like an acquaintance than a loved one. This was one of the most shocking parts of traveling for me. After you've been on the road for a few weeks you're thinking, “hey, I can't WAIT to get home and see everyone! Wait til they hear all of these stories! It's gonna be GREAT!”

Well, no, it probably won’t.

You see, people have their own day to day lives that don't involve you anymore. They haven't seen most of the places you have, they haven't driven a truck, they haven't lived on the road, and they simply cant relate to anything you've been through. They have their own concerns at work, at home, and with their friends. Your stories will interest them for a short bit, but they will soon want to get back to their own lives, of which you aren't really involved in anymore.

The other thing that surprised me right away about living on the road is the ENORMOUS amount of time you spend alone. And I mean ALONE. I'd estimate 20 out of every 24 hours each day you will be by yourself. You will pretty much never come across even one single person you know. It's a life of solitude and strangers. Waitresses, dock workers, and other drivers will be your main company.

The nice part is that truck stops are open 24 hours/day, 7 days/week. You can go inside anytime and have somebody to talk to. Anytime. There will be waitresses and other drivers in there and someone is always interested in a talk. Funny thing is, after years of being on the road I got used to this. I came off the road and bought my own house where I live alone.

I found myself going up to the local truck stop quite a bit because I was used to having people to sit and talk with anytime I liked. I missed it. So it just goes to show that you can learn to enjoy almost anything once you've gotten used to it.

Now the money part of over the road driving is great. With most companies you will get paid by the mile (there are some exceptions I'll discuss later) and will almost never, ever have to unload any freight. If you are willing to do a lot of driving and would like to make as much money as you can without burning yourself out, you can expect to make around $35,000-$45,000 your first year, and anywhere from $40,000-$55,000 from your second year on. The days are long, but all you really do is drive.

Because you actually live in the truck for weeks at a time, the equipment at any decent company is usually top notch. You should never have to drive a truck that is more than 3 years old, and good companies take excellent care of their equipment. They normally wont hesitate in the least when you request to get some work done. The truck pretty much stays in brand new condition.

Life on the road definitely takes A LOT of getting used to. But after a while you'll find that if the lifestyle suits you, it really is incredibly fun. We called ourselves “professional tourists”, which really is pretty accurate. You basically get paid to drive around the country in brand new rigs, see the sights, meet new people everyday, eat great food, and make great money.

If you decide to give up your apartment or home, which most people end up doing because you're paying for something you almost never use, you'll be able to save up tons of money because your only living expenses are food and fun. You have no rent, utilities, insurance, or car payments, so all that money just piles up in the bank.

Most companies will let you take your truck home with you, and if you're a good, safe, reliable driver and you kinda lay low, they'll let you use your tractor as your personal vehicle when you are at home, so you wont even need your own car.

Besides, when you come in to visit family and friends for a few days each month they will usually take you places or let you borrow their vehicle if need be. So living this lifestyle is a great way to save up a lot of money fast.

Lastly, over the road jobs are by far the easiest to find and have the lowest qualifications because they are hard jobs for the companies to fill. There just simply isn't enough people that are able or willing to live this lifestyle, at least not for long, so the companies are always desperate to fill these positions first. That's why they are usually the best paying and easiest jobs to find in the industry.

Regional

Ok, now regional jobs are a great option for many people. With regional jobs you are usually out 5 days a week and home on weekends. Now understand something: the freight you will be hauling is usually not predictable. Yes, there will be some customers that your company will have that will provide steady freight from one place to another on a rather predictable schedule.

But the vast majority of it will not be.

They will do their best to keep you moving during the week and get you home on time for the weekend but this is not always going to happen. Generally you can expect to get home sometime between Friday afternoon and Saturday morning. You will then be home around 36-48 hours. Often times you will bring a load home with you that will deliver on Monday morning, hopefully somewhere fairly close to your home.

Here's an example:

Say you live in Indianapolis, IN. After driving and making several deliveries all week, you may find yourself delivering a load on Friday morning in Nashville, TN. You then pick up a load Friday afternoon in Nashville that will deliver Monday morning in Chicago, IL. You pick up the load and head for home. You get home 7 a.m. Saturday morning. You live about 3 hours from Chicago, and the load is scheduled for 8 a.m. Monday.

You KNOW morning rush hour in Chicago is a nightmare so you want to arrive before 5 a.m. Your best bet is to leave late on Sunday evening, maybe 10 p.m., drive two hours, sleep at a truck stop outside of Chicago, and get up at 4 a.m. to arrive at the customer by 5 a.m. You can get a nap in for a couple of hours at the customer before they begin unloading you.

Job well done.

You were home from 7 a.m. Saturday until 10 p.m. Sunday. That is very, very typical of your home time schedule on a regional fleet.

As far as pay goes, there isn't too much difference between over the road and regional anymore. Over the past 10 years or so a lot of warehousing and production companies have divided up the country into regions in order to supply their customers with product faster and to save money on shipping charges. So instead of hauling auto parts say from Texas to Michigan, the factory may relocate part of its production to Indiana. Now the haul is much shorter.

This has opened up many more opportunities for regional driving jobs. The demand for regional jobs has increased significantly, and trucking companies have found a way to attract more drivers with the promise of very good pay and better home time.

The equipment for most regional jobs is about the same as most over the road jobs. You can expect fairly new vehicles that are very well maintained. The level of equipment will vary a bit more in this category though. Some companies will try to push older, less reliable equipment on drivers with the excuse that you will make great money and be home more often.

This is something you must decide for yourself as a driver. Test the market. There will be a number of companies in your area that offer the chance to be home each weekend. Sometimes you will have to make a trade-off between higher pay with an older truck or a little less pay with top notch equipment. You should not have to compromise on safety or reliability though.

Ask thoroughly about their maintenance program. Look at the trucks they have parked in the yard. If you see things like loose mirrors, cracked windshields, missing mud flaps, etc then obviously they aren't spending the time and money on maintenance that they should. I'll talk more about this later.

As far as job duties goes, there are a few more options when it comes to regional. In some cases you'll be asked to drive the truck and nothing else. You will simply get paid by the mile like over the road drivers do. Keep in mind that sometimes the miles you get each week can vary tremendously from week to week or from one company to another. Ask about their average weekly mileage per driver. Other jobs will involve a significant amount of unloading.

In fact you may make the bulk of your money unloading as opposed to just driving. If you are asked to unload trucks you should be able to make quite a bit more money per week than if you were just driving. This seems obvious, but with some companies it certainly is not the case. Do your homework.

I drove regional for several years. I actually made just as much money as I used to as an over the road driver, and when I took a regional job that involved a significant amount of unloading I made $15,000 per year more than with any over the road job I had ever had.

Regional is also an interesting mix of traveling and home time. You get the fun of living on the road and seeing the sites all week long, but then you get to enjoy your home time each weekend. You will be able to maintain a relationship, a home, a vehicle, and a social life while still making very good money. You wont be traveling as far from home as you would be while driving over the road.

Generally you'll cover an area within a radius of about 1000 miles from your home. Over the road you may have the opportunity to drive coast to coast. But even an area that large provides an interesting variety of places to go to which keeps it fun. I personally loved over the road when I was younger, but once I decided I wanted a home life regional was the perfect solution. Again, it just depends on what suits you the best.

Local

Finally there are local jobs. Local jobs generally involve being home everyday. You stay close to home and often times make several daily deliveries in your area. Local jobs can include dump trucks, dumpster trucks, food delivery trucks, and a whole slew of others.

Local driving provides the largest variety of choices when it comes to the type of driving, the type of job duties, and equipment you may use, including cranes, operating heavy machinery, pumping bulk fluids or liquids, or moving livestock.

Now you might be thinking, “hey, why spend so much time away from home when I can be home every night?” Well, a lot of people feel that way...and the principle of supply and demand kicks in. The greater the supply of drivers, the more difficult it is to find a job, and the lower the pay. Local jobs pay by far the least of the three types of jobs. The willingness to spend a lot of time away from home commands a much higher salary.

With such a variety of types of local jobs available there are opportunities to make a bit more money, but it will generally involve unloading. A good example is food delivery. Restaurants, gas stations, convenient stores, and bars all get deliveries several times per week. Generally these drivers are required to make anywhere from 5 to 20 deliveries per day and they do all the unloading, and sometimes even stock the shelves themselves. It can be very difficult, and at times even a bit dangerous.

Heavy lifting, walking through ice and snow, and walking up and down stairs and ramps are all part of daily life for these drivers. Injuries unfortunately are somewhat common. The constant lifting will get you into great shape, but definitely takes a couple months to really adapt to....a LONG couple of months.

The pay for these type of jobs will vary greatly. The easier jobs such as driving dump truck or most six wheel box trucks will generally be around $25,000. The more difficult jobs like food delivery where the driver puts in long hours unloading everyday can pay quite a bit better. Many are in the area of $35,000-$45,000 per year. But there are other things to beware of when you are considering a local driving job.

For starters, the days are often VERY long...anywhere from 10-15 hour days are common. Many drivers, myself included, come off the road at one time or another with aspirations of living a “normal” home life only to find that the only time you have at home is to eat, sleep, and shower. Eight to ten hours per day at home doesn't leave time for much of anything.

You realize you were making a whole lot more money getting home on weekends, didn't work as hard, and still had the same home and social life as you do now. But again, if you're married with children, try explaining to them why you're only home two days a week. Being a regional or over the road driver may not be an option, but at least you have the opportunity to make pretty good money driving locally if you're willing to work hard for it.

The other concern for local drivers is the conditions. Regional and over the road drivers spend the majority of their time on interstates, while local drivers are on regular streets full of stop lights, pedestrians, and heavy traffic all day long.

It obviously takes a tremendous amount of skill and attention to safely navigate local roads day in and day out. This is CERTAINLY not to say that the other forms aren't difficult or dangerous, but the hazards seem to come from all directions at all times on these local routes.

Lastly, because there is a larger pool of drivers to draw from on local jobs, often times the companies may require a bit more experience to qualify. This isn't always the case, but you should be aware of it.

Types Of Trucks

Ok, let's talk a little bit about your options for which type of trucks you can drive. Everybody has seen these trucks a million times, but there are a lot of points to consider when figuring out which one might be right for you.

Dry Van

A dry van trailer is the most common type of tractor trailer on the road. The trailer is simply a box on wheels, nothing more. You will haul anything and everything that can fit in the box and doesn't need temperature control. It could be food, clothing, auto parts, building supplies, etc. Almost anything. Even liquids in containers varying from buckets to drums to totes can be put in there. I'm telling ya, almost anything.

Dry van is the simplest form of tractor trailer job because there are really no specialized concerns unique to it. You don't need temperature control, you can't haul open liquids like a tanker can, you can't haul anything that needs to be dumped or pumped out, and you can't haul oversize loads. It's simply a matter of "throw it in the box and off you go". You may at times have to haul hazardous materials, but that isn't unique to dry van.

Because pay in any form of driving is partly based on specialized skills required and/or difficulty of doing the job, the only thing you will really find that will significantly boost your pay in this form of trucking is to take a job that requires you to load or unload, but this isn't too common.

All jobs may at times require what's called "driver assist" which can mean helping them unload somehow, but it's not too often and it's usually no bid deal. It may just mean counting the product going onto the trailer or moving pallets out of the way. No biggie. Most of the jobs which involve loading or unloading are local or regional jobs (mostly local).

There isn't much else to say about dry van. The other types of trucking jobs are more specialized, so we'll differentiate them here one at a time.

Flatbed

Flatbed drivers are in a click of their own. Their jobs involve more lifting and a bit more risk than most other types of trucking. There are several things to consider before taking a job doing this.

First of all..there's tarping your load. Any weather sensitive loads (and frustratingly enough some which aren't) need to be covered with a tarp. Now I have heard of some shippers which will tarp your load for you. Often times its because the manufacturer owns their own trucks and will tarp the loads they ship. But don't get your hopes up...it's rare.

Tarping a load is a HUGE pain in the neck. The tarps are huge and can easily weigh up to 100 pounds. A large part of the time you are simply outside in a parking lot without any protection from the weather "throwing a tarp" as they say. You take a heavy tarp and add rain, snow, ice, and mud, and you have one miserable job ahead of you. The tarps are a thick, rubber-based material which gets very stiff when it gets cold.

If your tarp gets wet and then freezes you'll have a layer of ice on it. Are you starting to see how much fun this can be? Most companies pay you to tarp the load, but whether or not it's worth the money for the trouble is something you have to decide from experience. My experience? No way.

Flatbeders are prone to injury more than most other types of drivers and the vast majority of them happen while throwing a tarp. The bed of the trailer is usually part aluminum and part wood. They put a few rows of oak boards down the length of the trailer to allow nails to be driven in to help secure the loads. Everyone has experienced the pleasure of trying to walk on wet, snow, or ice covered boards.

It's a nightmare.

Well, as you can surely imagine, the aluminum portion of the trailer is no better. Most injuries occur while trying to lift something heavy, falling off the trailer, or while trying to use a “cheater bar” to get leverage while cranking down on the ratchet straps. Back and shoulder injuries are most common, while falling off a trailer can lead to all sorts of injuries to your head, knees, ankles, elbows, and hips.

Now don't misunderstand me...I'm not saying you WILL have these accidents and injuries. There are a large number of drivers who haven't...but there are plenty who have. It's just a big part of flatbedding you have to be aware of.

Oversize and overweight loads are another concern. For whatever reason (I'd guess because they seem to get away with it) companies often don't pay anything extra for hauling an oversize load. But there is a lot to be aware of when it comes to hauling these loads. Every state has different rules regarding them, but there are some generalities than can be made.

Oversize loads often can not be moved at night or in poor weather. This is by law in many states. Depending on the size of the load and the state you are in you may or may not need an escort vehicle, or several of them. The really large or heavy loads often need police escort. You will also need special permits at times in each state you drive through. Your company will handle getting these permits for you but they will have to be faxed to you at a truck stop or at the shipper.

You can be almost certain that every weigh station you come to will carefully check your weight and ask you to come inside to show them your permits. One small problem and you will be shut down on the spot until your company gets whatever it is you require.

Also, finding a parking spot in the evening at a truck stop is difficult enough when you CAN fit into a parking spot.

Needing two spots or parking along the edge of the lot because you are over length can really be tough. The handling of oversize loads will vary from company to company and should be a priority when you inquire into employment.

The DOT is another concern for flatbedders. The DOT LOVES FLATBEDS! There are numerous regulations with regard to strapping down your load based on the weight, size, and breakup of the load. Some loads will be on pallets, maybe 20 or so, and some may be just one piece of machinery.

Depending on a number of factors you will be required to strap or chain down the load every so many feet and with a certain amount of holding strength.

The DOT loves flatbeds because there are so many opportunities for them to find a problem. Your straps may be worn, loose, or not of the proper rating. Your tarp may be loose or have loose cords hanging. You may not have enough straps or chains for your load and so on. They can see your load at a glance and often tell right away if they can get you on something. As a flatbedder you will get a lot of scrutiny.

So as you can see, there are a number of issues specific to hauling loads on a flatbed trailer. Because of this, flatbedders tend to be paid quite well. Often times a flatbed driver can make anywhere from $5,000-$15,000 per year more than someone hauling a dry van or refrigerated trailer.

Also, flatbedders are like a little fraternity within the industry and many drivers really like the unique challenges and better pay that come with it.

Refrigerated Trailers (Reefers)

Refrigerated trailers aren't too much different these days than hauling a dry van in a lot of ways but there are a few specifics to be aware of. Modern units (reefer unit) are very well built and reliable. They automate the temperature much as a refrigerator or furnace would in your home.

You simply set the temperature and it takes care of the rest. Often times reefers are used to protect a product from freezing and thus are capable of heating or cooling the trailer.

The reefer unit will have some indicator on it, usually a series of lights, which can easily be seen through your mirror as you are driving to indicate whether the unit is functioning properly. Generally a green, yellow, or red light will let you know how the unit is functioning. It takes very little extra effort to simply maintain a certain temperature in the trailer.

You simply set the temperature on the unit with the keypad and keep fuel in the unit's fuel tank. Once in a while you will have a problem with one of the units and will have to take the trailer to a reefer repair shop to have it looked at. Your company will advise you on this.

Reefer companies haul a lot of food as you would expect. They also haul a variety of products which may or may not require temperature control, like some hazardous materials. However you will often find yourself hauling the same products you would be hauling in a regular dry van. You aren't limited to temperature-sensitive products but they do tend to pay more to the company hauling them so they try to get a temperature-sensitive load if they can find one.

The main difference between hauling a reefer and hauling other types of trailers involves the type of driving you do. Produce loads are the bread and butter of the reefer industry. "The Valley" in California is one of the richest produce areas in the world.

Tons and tons of produce comes out of California everyday heading all over the country. Because of this, a lot of reefer companies try to get you out to California as often as possible and the average run tends to be much longer than those in other forms of trucking.

However it is quite common to have to make several small pickups in different parts of California and hauling them across the country to their destination. Anywhere from 3-8 pickups is quite common. This can be very time consuming and tiring.

You will likely get paid maybe $10-$20 per extra pickup, but when you consider it takes you an entire day rather than a couple hours to pick up a load you usually would rather just make one pickup and get rolling.

The other problem comes at the delivery. Most of these loads go to some sort of grocery warehouse or farmer's market. Getting the trailer unloaded requires your company to pay somebody to do it. I never could understand why grocery deliveries were the driver's responsibility to get unloaded. Almost no other type of freight will work this way.

You have to hire a "lumper", which is generally a group of guys that have their own independent company hired by the warehouse or market.

The trucking company will actually pay the money, not the driver, but the driver has to handle the transaction. These grocery warehouses also don't seem to mind making you wait 6-12 hours on the average before they will even begin to unload you...another day wasted.

If you've never had to deal with grocery warehouses, this may not sound like any big deal, but BELIEVE ME, it is the most thoroughly aggravating thing you will deal with in the reefer industry. Many, many drivers have switched from reefer to dry van jobs because they just couldn't stand one more day sitting in the parking lot of a grocery warehouse waiting to be unloaded.

It wears you out after a while.

The pay difference between reefer and dry van is minimal. You generally will pick one or the other because of personal preference, not pay. Some people like the longer runs and traveling coast to coast with the reefer companies, while some prefer the shorter runs and greater home time you can generally find with a dry van. Not having to deal with grocery warehouses is also a bonus for dry van drivers.

Tankers -> After gaining experience.

Driving a tanker is quite different from the other types of driving in a number of significant ways, many of which revolve around your driving skills and the type of tanker. You have 3 major types of tankers...food grade, non-food grade, and bulk solids.

Food grade tankers do not have baffles in them. Baffles are walls, sometimes solid and sometimes with holes in them, which act either to divide the tanker into compartments or to minimize the sloshing of the liquid within the tank.

Because of the health issues involved with keeping the tank clean and sanitized they do not allow baffles inside the tank to prevent sloshing. You can compartmentalize a food tanker, but you can not prevent sloshing with barriers.

A typical food-grade tanker can haul about 48,000 pounds of liquid. You can imagine the forces involved if you were to haul a very thin, heavy liquid, like salt water, which only fills the tank half way before you are maxed out on weight. When you accelerate or hit the brakes the liquid will slosh from front to rear. If you are not gentle it can be very dangerous.

For instance, if you are exiting the interstate onto an off ramp with a sharp curve and you hit the brakes pretty hard just before the curve, the liquid will surge forward and give you a huge jolt (hard enough to knock the hat off your head) right in the center of the curve. It could easily cause a rollover or cause you to slide off the ramp if the road is slick. The sloshing can also make shifting much more difficult which takes a bit of time to get used to.

Non-food grade tanks are allowed to have baffles in them to prevent sloshing so this is a bit of an advantage, but I wouldn't call it night and day. Let's call it a little bit better. The trade-off of course is that you are hauling chemicals, often very dangerous ones.

The difference in pay between chemical and food-grade jobs is negligible so I never really could understand why someone would choose to haul dangerous chemicals instead of things like milk, honey, and juice.

You can't mix food-grade with non-food-grade loads in the same tanker. You must haul either one or the other type of product by law. Now of course one company can own both types of tanks and have their drivers switch between them, but honestly I don't know of any companies that do this. They may be out there, but generally a company will specialize in one or the other.

Dry bulk tanks haul things like sugar, flower, and sand. These dry bulk materials require special tanks and air-pump systems in them to unload the product. The difference in pay between the three different types of tanks really is negligible so again it's really a matter of preference.

Now all three types of tanks will require a bit of work from the driver. Often times you will be required to at least hook up hoses from your tanker to the shipper or receiver's tanks. Sometimes you will have a pump installed on your trailer and will be required to pump the product out of your tank into the receiver's tank.

You must also vent your tank which usually just means to open the hatch on top or the tank will collapse as you unload it. Air must be able to fill the space that was occupied by the product, just like if you were dumping out a gallon jug of water.

Most companies pay you a little something...maybe $30-$50 dollars....if you have to pump out your tank. Depending on the type of tanker and product the process can take anywhere from 45 minutes to 2 hours to complete and it really isn't difficult or dangerous.

Now with a chemical tanker, if you have a hazardous chemical the receiver may ask you to wait in a safe area within the complex while qualified and well-equipped workers unload the product.

Another unique aspect of hauling a tanker is the fact that you must go to a tank wash and get your tanker washed out after every load, unless you are hauling the exact same product again. Larger companies will try to save time and money by having spare tanks at the tank washes that you can just swap out and keep rolling.

They may also try to get you back to back loads of the same product if possible. But if you work for a small company you will usually have to get the tank washed after every load.

This can take several hours at best or an entire wasted day at worst to accomplish. Since you are generally getting paid by the mile or by the load you don't want to waste time this way. Some companies will pay you a little bit for your time while you're getting a tank washed, but the small amount of money isn't worth the time.

Now there are some unique advantages to hauling a tanker that I really enjoyed. For starters, you are ALWAYS heavy. Now this is a small disadvantage when dealing with mountains, but in the winter time the extra weight really significantly helps the truck hold the road.

Another advantage is that you don't have to worry about individual axle weights because the liquid will balance itself. Getting the axle weights to balance evenly can be a real hassle with other forms of trucking. Not having to deal with axle weights is a nice bonus.

The tanks, especially the liquid tanks, are much shorter than other types of trailers which means you don't have to worry too much about going under low bridges.

Now DON'T GET CRAZY here.

It's not that you can't hit a bridge, but you are about a foot shorter than a standard trailer and the foot is a HUGE difference.

I was pretty happy about that too.

Finally, the round tank is much nicer in the wind than a flat-sided trailer. This really is a very big deal especially when you are empty. You might not expect a big rig to get blown around that easily in the wind but you may soon find out otherwise. Driving an empty rig feels like you're driving a sailboat down the road especially in winds about 25 mph or so.

So as you can probably tell I'm quite fond of pulling a tanker, especially a food-grade tanker. There are some nice advantages to it but please be forewarned...the sloshing liquid can be extremely dangerous if you're not careful. It may not be the best place to start as a brand new driver, but it is certainly worth considering after you get a bit of experience under your belt.

Dump Trucks

The last separate category I'd like to talk about is dump trucks. I wanted to mention a few important points about these trucks in particular because they are so common and yet are surprisingly dangerous in a number of ways you may not be aware of.

First let me mention one minor point. Trucking companies which have 18 wheelers DO NOT consider dump trucks as driving experience per say. When those companies mention experience they generally only consider other 18 wheelers as experience. I personally think this is a huge mistake on their part.

To safely navigate a large dump truck day in and day out can be just as difficult, if not MORE difficult, than an 18 wheeler. If I was hiring someone for a job in an 18 wheeler I would be quite happy to find someone with safe dump trucking experience. Let's take a look at why that is.

First of all, the maximum gross weight of an 18 wheeler is 80,000 pounds. A tri-axle dump truck can gross nearly the same in most states, maybe a few thousand pounds less. Yet a dump truck only has 3 rear axles with brakes on them, an 18 wheeler has four. Believe me it makes a difference in stopping power.

Secondly, a dump truck usually carries loads with a MUCH higher center of gravity which makes them much easier to tip over.

Thirdly, a dump truck is often operated in off-road conditions. If you can handle a 72,000 pound dump truck with a high center of gravity on a hilly, soft dirt road or driveway, you can handle anything. Not to mention you have to find stable, level ground to be able to hold you upright while you are dumping that load. Not at all an easy task.

Lastly, like any local job, dump trucks are operated on normal streets in stop and go conditions. They are extremely heavy, not the easiest to stop sometimes, have a high center of gravity, and traffic is flying all around you. This is no easy job let me tell you.

Finally, the pay is usually pretty lousy and the hours are quite unpredictable. The work is quite seasonal in the northern parts of the country also. You can usually expect anywhere from $10-$16 per hour with the number of hours worked in a week ranging from zero in the winter to 70 or more during good weather weeks in the summer.

Because of the difficulty of handling these vehicles I don't recommend this type of job for a brand new driver. It can be done, but I would be more comfortable having a driver start out in a vehicle with a little bit less to worry about.

Doubles And Triples

We've all seen the double trailers and in some places triple trailer combinations. I'm not going into this area of trucking in this book because I am gearing this book toward drivers that are new to the industry. Doubles and triples can be extremely dangerous to handle especially on slick roads.

Most of these companies will not, and SHOULD not, allow a brand new driver the opportunity to drive these trucks.

If by chance you do find a company that will I STRONGLY suggest you get experience driving a standard tractor trailer for at least one full year before considering making this move. These companies have excellent pay, benefits, and home time packages but again, the truck is extremely difficult to handle under adverse conditions.

Please do not consider taking one of these opportunities with less than one year under your belt. Please.

Choosing Your First Company

As you probably realize there are tens or even hundreds of thousands of trucking companies nationwide. There are some as small as one truck and some as large as tens of thousands of trucks. There are local, regional, and over the road companies and some that are a combination of two or even all three. There are tanker, flat bed, reefer, dry van, dump, and a multitude of other types of trucks you can drive.

There are companies that specialize in one type and companies that have a combination of several different types. So with all of these choices presented to you how do you know where to start your career? To tell you the truth it's not that hard. Let's cover some of the key points you should focus on.

First let's start with your lifestyle. Are you married? Divorced? Do you have children? Do you love adventure? Would you like to travel extensively and see the country or have you already had that chance and want to stay near home?

Home time is one of the most important considerations you should make. There is one point I can not stress enough – if you have a family of your own, please, please, please don't take an over the road job where you are gone for weeks at a time.

It's been done by thousands of drivers over the years and is being done by thousands today, but the stress it puts on every member of the family is enormous and is simply not necessary. There are tons of opportunities in the industry to make good money and be home at least every weekend, often times every night.

Countless numbers of families have split up because of the time apart. I certainly don't want to see that number grow.

Even regional jobs can be very stressful, but I think it can be done. It will definitely test your relationship both as a couple and with your children though. Ideally you would like to be home with your family everyday but often times your financial situation dictates that you get a really good paying job which you may not be able to find in a local company.

Be forewarned though, even a regional job will be a HUGE test of your family's strength, not to mention you will miss so much of your family's lives.

You may be married, or in a serious relationship, but you don't have any children. There are a lot of couples that travel together. In some cases both are drivers and share the driving duties, in other cases only one drives and the other helps in varying degrees with navigation, phone calls, paperwork, and in a variety of other duties.

But again be forewarned... the inside of your truck is the size of a walk-in closet and you two will be together nearly non-stop 24 hours a day, seven days a week.

I don't know if you've ever tried to share a tiny space with another person practically ever minute of every day but it is very difficult. At best it will take a lot of getting used to and at worst you will be at each other's throats after a while. Some couples can handle it, many can't.

Often times the only way to find out is to try it. But if you do decide to give it a shot please don't give up your home or apartment for several months figuring it will work out. If you can handle it for three months you should be ok.

Often though both parties are glad that they can travel together sometimes and at other times one person can stay home to give themselves a break and to take care of other responsibilities. There really is no easy answer for this type of situation. It's a matter of trial and error.

Now when I started driving I was 21 years old, hadn't traveled too much, had never been married, and had no children. The idea of traveling all of the time and living in the truck sounded AWESOME, and it was!

The better part of my first 9 years of driving was over the road. I would stay on the road for weeks and sometimes months at a time. I just totally loved it! It really suited my personality and lifestyle. I was able to give up my apartment and vehicle and just let the money pile up in the bank.

I usually found myself driving a lot during the week and having a lot of free time on the weekends to entertain myself. I'd go to bars, sporting events, concerts, and do the "tourist thing" like in Las Vegas or New Orleans. It was spectacular!

So your first consideration should be home time. But please be honest with yourself. Don't convince yourself to do something that deep down inside you probably have some serious doubts about. If you have a family please try to find a job with as much home time as possible.

If you absolutely NEED to make as much money as possible at least for a little while then at least try to formulate a solid plan that will get you out of your money crunch and into a position to take a job that will get you home as often as possible. I'm telling you, too much time away from home can ruin a family. Try to avoid it.

The next big consideration will be the size of the company you choose to work for. I have worked for companies with over 5,000 trucks and for companies with as few as four. It's a huge cultural difference.

The larger companies have a huge amount of resources available. They have tons and tons of different types of freight and driving opportunities. They often have local jobs, dedicated jobs - where you remain with one customer or run one route all the time, regional jobs, and over the road.

They have much more flexibility when it comes to home time and will allow you to freely move between different divisions within the company when you feel an opportunity presents itself.

Larger companies also have accounts set up with customers, lumpers, repair shops, towing companies, motels, bus companies, and truck stops. These accounts generally allow you to walk in the door, tell them who you work for, and get what you need taken care of without doing a thing.

Repairs, towing, showering, getting bus tickets when needed, and picking up or delivering freight becomes much faster and easier under this system.

To me this was always a really big deal.

Larger companies also have a large pool of equipment to use. A variety of tractors to choose from and a huge number of additional trailers available make life much nicer for the driver. With the extra trailers you get to do a lot of "drop and hooks" where you pull into the customer, drop your trailer, grab a different trailer, and leave. You don't have to wait around to be loaded or unloaded.

This is really huge because most jobs pay by the mile so the time you spend sitting around waiting to load or unload is unpaid, wasted time. You want to keep rolling as much as possible and drop and hooks can help you make a lot more money in a lot less time.

Drop and hooks also give you more flexibility as far as when you make your pickups and deliveries. Often times they will give you a deadline to pickup or deliver but you can generally get in there as early as you like, 24 hours a day.

So if you have to pick up a load that's sitting in a trailer in downtown Chicago you don't have to try to push through rush hour traffic to arrive at a certain time. You can go in late at night when traffic is light. Or maybe you're gonna get there really early but you really would love to take a nap for an hour or two or sit down for a nice meal first.

Go for it!

As long as you arrive ahead of the deadline everyone is happy. Believe me you're gonna LOVE having this kind of flexibility.

To continue with this theme larger companies tend to have a long list of perks.

I've worked for companies that had things like free family counseling, large plush driver facilities with arcades, big screen TVs, and restaurants, free 24 hour medical phone lines where you can call and talk to nurses confidentially about any medical questions you might have, discounts on travel accommodations, top of the line health insurance, 401k and direct deposit, free high speed wireless networks, shower facilities, and on and on and on.

I must say at times we'd wish they would just pay us more instead, but you know how that goes. The perks really are unbelievable though.

Ok so large companies must have some disadvantages right? Of course they do. At a large company you are simply a number not a name. You hopefully will get to know a few people working in the offices like your dispatcher, his or her boss, and maybe one or two middle managers like a terminal manager or operations manager.

If you get to know that many people... and by get to know I mean they actually recognize you by name or truck number, you've probably done either an excellent job or a terrible job over a period of many months or more likely a couple of years.

It's tough to stand out when there are thousands of drivers at one company. So if you like that personal attention and family-type atmosphere a large company is not going to provide what you're looking for.

Because of this you will find it very difficult to get any special consideration for anything. Doing a great job for a couple of years is going to get you an automated thank you letter and maybe a patch for the company jacket you had to buy from your own company when you wanted one.

On the other end of things you may find yourself in a situation that nobody will take the time to understand your side of. They don't have the time and frankly they really don't care. I'm going to go deeper into this subject later on with a few stories related to this theme.

Smaller companies in my opinion don't have too many advantages over the larger ones from a driver's perspective. You will definitely get to know everyone in the office and they will certainly know you. Often times if you live nearby your main office the people in your company will even get to know your family and the families of the other employees.

This family atmosphere is nice in a way, but you also have to be aware of a couple things.

For one, just like in any tight group of people, everyone tends to know everyone else's business. Maybe you don't want everyone at work knowing about an operation you have to have, or the tough times you're having with your marriage, or the trouble your kid got into at school.

Maybe you got a well deserved raise but now the other drivers are envious and raising a fuss. Or maybe your excellent performance is being rewarded with more miles and a nicer truck which again causes problems with the other drivers.

As you can probably tell I've been in these type of situations before and I'm not really too fond of them.

The other concern with regard to company size is how much your company counts on you. At a large company if you'd like to take some time off nobody really cares. I've taken MONTHS off at times and simply been told, "ok just turn your truck in to the terminal and let us know when you're ready to return and we'll get ya goin."

But at a really small company that's not likely to happen. You may be one of ten drivers so if you take time off they just lost 10% of their fleet! The smaller companies rely on you much more so than a big company does so you don't have as much flexibility.

One time I worked for a small company pulling food-grade tankers. There were only eleven drivers in the company. I ran really, really hard for them and they got a little too greedy about it. It got to the point that I was running an average of about 4500 miles per week. That's a lot!

As time went on the owner expected more and more. It was getting ridiculous. Finally I stayed out on the road for almost six straight weeks, averaged about 4500 miles per week, and when I returned home he booked a load for me to haul two days later. Six weeks on the road, two days at home, and I have to leave again? I don't think so.

Well, he fired me.

I had been there a year and had a perfect safety and service record. I also was second in average miles driven per week but I guess that wasn't good enough. Turns out the owner was in serious financial trouble and I found out the company closed just a few months later.

So it turns out that he was desperate to get all the money coming in he could get to save the company. But he had a good thing going with me and ruined it. Don't you make the same mistake. Don't run so hard you'll damage you mind, your body, or your license. Think long-term and make smart choices.

Just be aware that small companies will count on you far more than large companies will. There will be advantages and disadvantages to any company you work for. It's always somewhat of a compromise. It's just a matter of finding what works for you.

One of the best ways in my opinion to really find out what life is like on the inside of a company you are considering applying to is to talk with some of the drivers and mechanics that work there. You'll be pleasantly surprised at the honesty you'll get.

Now please be aware of one thing though... often times a company will offer a referral bonus to any employee that refers a driver to the company. Often times it's quite significant.. in the area of $500.

So when you begin talking with a driver or mechanic make it perfectly clear that you are looking for an honest opinion, not a sales pitch. If you were looking for propaganda you could simply talk to their recruiting department.

If they want to give you their name and truck number so they can make money for recruiting you simply thank them for their time and try to find someone else.

But most of the time you will get a brutally honest opinion. Drivers often tend to look out for other drivers. We all live the same kind of lives and face the same difficulties so the last thing we should want to do is make life difficult for one another.

I've been asked many hundreds of times about my experience working for a particular company. I have never once given out my truck number or name, nor have I ever received a nickel in referral money. Often times guys were so appreciative of my time and honesty that they asked ME for the info knowing I would get paid for the referral and I politely declined.

I told them there was no way they could be sure I was being honest with them if I knew I was going to get paid to promote my company. I've gotten plenty of good advice for free over the years so I just considered it good karma to give some back.

Make sure you talk to at least five different drivers from any particular company. One or two could by coincidence be happy or unhappy with a company at any given time but if you can get a pretty consistent group of opinions from several different drivers then you know you've probably gotten a good feel for the way drivers are being treated there.

Ask them if they're getting the mileage they would like to be getting, whether they get home when they are supposed to, and whether or not the trucks are well maintained. That's the three most important things a company must do well.

Also talk to one or two mechanics. The biggest thing you'd like to know is if the maintenance program is a good one. Ask them if the trucks are well taken care of and especially if a driver's requests for small things like new wiper blades, faulty mirror heaters, and blown fuses are handled promptly and without debate.

If they aren't taking the time and care to look after the trucks then not only will you be losing a lot of money while unreliable trucks are sitting in the repair shop all of the time but you'll know that the company's management really isn't concerned with the comfort, safety, and happiness of its drivers.

A poor maintenance program is a huge red flag. Stay away from that company.

Also, be leery of guarantees from a company. The trucking industry is by nature cyclical and unpredictable. If they make promises like "you WILL be home every Friday by dinnertime", or "everybody gets home for the holidays", or "you WILL get a minimum of 2000 miles per week" then you KNOW you're being lied to.

There are no guarantees in this industry. Weather factors, fleet size, economic fluctuations, vehicle breakdowns, gaining or losing customers, changes in computer software or dispatching structure, and a massive number of other variables all lead to a naturally unpredictable amount of miles and home time from week to week and year to year.

Staying with the theme of "beware guarantees", let me warn you about company recruiters. A recruiter's job is to get you in the door...period. Once you've gotten hired at a company their job is done. They will lie their heads off if it gets them paid...like used car salespeople.

Tons of drivers I've talked to have been promised new trucks, certain divisions, big miles, and lots of home time only to find out they've been lied to by the recruiter.

What can you do about it if this happens to you? Nothing.

Everyone will simply shrug their shoulders and say, "don't know what to tell ya". There's one easy way to test a recruiter...tell them to put it in writing. If they promise you a new truck tell them to fax it in writing to you with their name on it so that you can bring it to orientation with you.

If they'll do that you may actually get what they promised...but I'm not guaranteeing that either. Recruiting can be a dirty process at times.... so watch out for promises.

They will lie to you if they think they can get away with it.

There will be good weeks and bad ones, good months and bad ones, even years can fluctuate quite bit from one to the next. You have to take the good with the bad and try to get a good understanding of the big picture and how all of the different variables will affect your mileage and home time.

If a company makes guarantees, they're lying.

If they make statements like, "we try to get everyone home on weekends and holidays", and "you'll average about 2200 miles per week overall" then you can be pretty sure that they're doing their best to be honest.

Just be aware of the personal interests and possible agenda of the person you are talking with. Remember, you as a driver are the one in demand. You should be interviewing the company, not the other way around. You know if your record is decent then they'll be glad to have you. Make sure they are offering what you are looking for in a company. You may not have ever been in this position before.

Up to this point in your life maybe you were hoping to get a job and were competing for positions. It's not that way in the trucking industry. They need you far more than you need them. Don't let them try to convince you otherwise.

Getting Trained On The Road

Ok so now you've made it through your schooling, you have your CDL, you found the company you want to work for, and you've gotten hired. Congratulations! Your first job in your new career. You're going to be excited as hell at this point, and you should be. You worked hard at school, you spent the money, passed the tests, and here you are.... you've certainly earned it!

Congratulations!

Now let's cover what you can expect from your training period. Mine I'm happy to say went very well. So here we go.

Once you get hired you will be paired up with an experienced driver and you will travel together as a team in the same truck for an average of about four to six weeks. If the trainer feels you are ready to handle your own truck he will return with you to the main terminal where you will be issued your own truck and you will be on your own from then on.

The personality and attitude of your trainer will mean everything! I mentioned earlier that you will sometimes come across these cocky, hardcore, authoritarian idiots that take themselves WAY too seriously.

If you see you have one of these types you can often times request a different trainer. But give him/her a week or so. He/she may have just been having a bad day when you two first met.

When you get hired on at a company try to request a trainer that has a reputation for being tolerant, pleasant, and patient. Learning to drive is quite stressful, not to mention the other factors like time away from home and learning all of the rules from state to state.

A patient, pleasant trainer will make your experience a thousand times more beneficial and enjoyable for you.

My trainer was absolutely awesome! He was a laid-back, intelligent, pleasant guy who clearly enjoyed life on the road and the chance to teach new drivers the ropes. We laughed a lot and talked all the time about everything from driving to our philosophies of life, love, and the pursuit of happiness. It really went well.

He told me right away he only had two rules... one, if he tells me to do something while I'm driving please do it right away even if it doesn't make sense to me at the time. He explained that with his experience he may be able to spot something that I'm yet unaware of so just do what he asks right away and then we can talk about it all day afterwards. Made perfect sense to me.

The second rule... if you are driving while I am in the back sleeping and you drive off a cliff, DON'T scream and wake me up.... I don't want to know what's coming! I really got a kick out of that one. He had a great sense of humor and we had a great time.

I remember walking up to the truck, getting in the passenger side and introducing myself. I couldn't BELIEVE I had made it to this point and was actually getting ready to head out on the highway! We were in Atlanta, GA and I threw my duffel bag in the sleeper and asked him if he knew where we were going first. He said, "yap, we're starting with a short trip to Maryland." A SHORT TRIP TO MARYLAND????

To me a short trip was to a gas station... in GEORGIA! Atlanta, even! But to a veteran driver a 500 or 600 mile trip is nothing more than a simple everyday thing. But to me it was the start of a whole new life....and what a life it has turned out to be!

He told me the company wanted every student to have at least one trip to the northeast and one trip to California while in training. He was going to try to convince them that Maryland was far enough to the northeast and from there he was hoping we could go out west.

OK, I WAS FREAKIN! CALI-FREAKIN-FORNIA?????

We're gonna DRIVE to CALIFORNIA????

I mean, I knew that's what my job would be as a truck driver but dreaming about it and being told you're about to really DO it is two totally different things! Holy cow I should have brought a diaper! No, wait, I'm ok. Ok this is GREAT! Wow what a day!

So sure enough we headed out to Maryland. He drove the first hour or so and then pulled into a rest area and asked if I felt like I was ready to drive. I really felt I was. My first REAL time behind the wheel as an official truck driver. Only 21 years old! Wow, what a day!

I took off, went through the gears, aimed for the horizon, and there we were.... gone with the wind! I was smiling from ear to ear. I just couldn't believe it was real. But sure enough it was. Wow.

He was very patient and said very little for a while. He just wanted me to relax and concentrate on the road. It was easy, really. Not much traffic, open interstate, cruise control, and a warm sunny early evening in Northern Georgia in the fall. Amazing.

I drove for a couple hours and as we got closer to Charlotte, NC and the sun went down we pulled into a truck stop to get some dinner. I was really livin it. I didn't stop smiling for a week I swear! But there were going to be a couple of tough times ahead. Not that day, but soon enough. Luckily I had a great trainer.

A new driver was bound to make some mistakes, and I did. But he got us through em like a champ and to this day I really appreciate the way he handled things.

The first mistake came a few days later in Ohio. I was following a state route toward Toledo and he said he was going to take a short nap. He told me to just keep following that route and he'd be up in a little bit. I had no problem with it....or so I thought.

The first minor incident came when I saw an option I was unfamiliar with... the state route or the business route. I took the business route and right away it exited us off the main highway. I was hoping I could get turned back without him noticing but he had great senses. He woke up and popped his head through the curtain.

I explained what happened and he wasn't concerned at all. I turned around and continued on. But about an hour later when he woke up I was cruising down the same highway and he asked, "where are we?" and I said, "still on the same highway". Well we were on the same highway but we were no longer following the proper route. The route number I was supposed to be following made a turn in a different direction and I didn't know it could do that!

I just thought a highway was a certain route and you just kept going straight! Well, turns out I was wrong and we were about 100 miles out of route.

He was slightly irked for a moment I could tell but he didn't say much of anything. He just looked at the map and found us a new route. It took us a bit longer to get there, but we were there plenty early for our appointment the next morning. Job successfully completed, no harm done, and a lesson well learned.

He knew little mistakes like that were common with new drivers and the whole thing was forgotten. I was glad for that.

The next day I still felt bad and so I voluntarily took his cleaning supplies and thoroughly cleaned the entire inside of the truck while he was inside the truck stop showering. He was pleasantly surprised when he returned to find his truck spotlessly clean and I explained how much I appreciated his patience.

He said not to think anything of it, that of all of the serious things that can go wrong out here, to go a little bit off course was no concern to him whatsoever. Man was I relieved.

The next incident came at a drive-thru truck wash at one of our terminals in the Midwest. It was a narrow passage and I was driving through it and veered a bit off course, scraping the steps on the side of the truck against the guide rail. OH NO WHAT HAVE I DONE NOW???? Well, he looked at it, laughed a bit, and said not to worry about it. They would fix it up quick. So I drove it over to our shop and they just bent the step back into place.

Again, another minor incident but my trainer handled it much better than I. Patience is everything when you're teaching someone something let me tell ya! Incident forgotten.

The next event that stands out in my mind wasn't a screw up on my part this time. Instead it was a hard lesson on the harsh realities of the road. A lesson I would never forget.

I was sleeping while he was driving and woke up when I noticed he was stopping. I asked if we were done driving and he said no that there was an accident ahead. I came up into the front seat and saw all the emergency lights flashing in the night sky. As we got up to it we noticed there was only one car pulled off to the side but a lot of police and fire trucks blocking the right lane. We soon saw why... there was a bunch of debris in the road. As we came along side of it we saw a sneaker on the road and a piece of clothing. What we saw next was beyond belief.... it looked as if a deer had been hit and splattered into bloody chunks all over the road.

But that wasn't a deer...it was a person.

Welcome to life on the road. A deafening silence had came over us. We drove silently for about half an hour and he pulled off to go to sleep. We didn't really talk about it much after that.

We didn't really need to.

After all, what was there that needed to be said? Accidents on the highway can happen without warning and without mercy. The events seem to happen instantaneously and often brutally. One moment everything is wonderful, the next moment....well, for some there is no next moment.

That one moment is sometimes the last moment...and that's that....no do-overs....no anything.

It's amazing how one thing can be so many different things to so many different people. The same road can be a path to a whole new life for so many people one day...and a graveyard for others the next. A week on the road can feel like a month sometimes because you see and do so much in such a short amount of time.

So far I had only been on the road for just a few short days and already I felt very different. My new career as a truck driver had just begun and already It was clear that life on the road was going to be an amazing and unpredictable journey unlike anything that had come before.

So with that incident behind us a new day began and we were forced to try to forget about it. After all, none of the other options were going to lead us anywhere good. So on we went.

We got our trip to California. I had never been west of Ohio and couldn't believe the amazing scenery we passed along the way. The trip out there took several days and I enjoyed every incredible minute of it. When we got out to the rockies in Wyoming the scenery seemed straight out of a movie about the old west.

Well, DUH!

It WAS the west of course but television was the only way I had ever seen it.

It seemed liked a dream. It was hard to imagine that you could leave the oak and maple covered mountains of the east, go across the endless corn fields of the Midwest, then cross the high desert and Rocky Mountains of the west, and come down out of those rocky mountains into one of the most fertile valleys in the world in central California all in just a few days time and you're still in the same country!!!

From sea to shining sea, indeed.

The beauty of this country can not be understood or conveyed through pictures, or in words, or in song. You can meditate, speculate, and postulate day and night but until you've traveled these highways yourself and have seen this land with your own eyes you know nothing of America The Beautiful.

The song was written from the experience of someone who had seen this great land not because they thought they could convey to others what they had seen, but because they so desperately wished they could and just couldn't bear the agony of not trying.

Our land is truly something to behold.

I spent a total of two weeks with my trainer. I don't think he could have done his job any better than he did. There weren't any more incidents that I can recall and I'd have to say those two weeks were a complete success. I was fortunate enough several years later to cross paths with him again in a truck stop in central Ohio. He remembered me and I was quite happy to tell him how thankful I was for the knowledge he had passed on to me and the patience with which he had done it.

I told him I gave him credit for being a big part of the reason I had had several years of safe driving under my belt and he was quite appreciative of the gesture. I never saw him again after that but to be honest I never expected to. It was truly a miracle that we had even crossed paths that one last time and for that I was very thankful.

It's not often you get to learn important lessons from people that last you a lifetime and years later get to thank them for it. This was one time I was just really lucky to have that chance.

If you attend a private school, your trainer may be the first person who gets to teach you the REAL way things are done on the road. What the hell do I mean by that? Well, schools are simply a place you attend to acquire enough knowledge to be given a job. The vast majority of the skills you will learn in any trade will be learned on the job. What knowledge your trainer will give you will depend a lot upon his attitude and approach.

Some trainers are hardcore company men that believe in teaching everything strictly by the book. If the law says you have only two hours of driving available before needing a ten hour break but you have three hours left to your destination a hardcore trainer may insist that you stop after two hours. The reality for most drivers is that you get the job done and get to your destination if you feel you can do it safely.

Both types of schools really have little choice but to teach things strictly by the book. They are scrutinized and would be in all kinds of trouble if they were found to be teaching you ways to cheat the logbook or run with a load that is slightly overweight. But life is simply not that black and white.

For starters, you are being paid by the mile. The more miles you run the more money you make. So when faced with the choice of continuing to run even though you are out of hours or giving up that paycheck and shutting down the truck, often times you aren't going to want to give up the money to sit around and watch TV at a truck stop.

You want to make all the money you can make...safely.

Another example would be if you loaded a load that had to go 500 miles and you knew you might be overweight but there were no weigh stations along your route. The shipper that just loaded you is closing in an hour and you cant get back there to get the extra weight taken off in time.

What do you do?

Do you run the load anyways and make the money or shut down until the next day so they can remove the extra weight and lose an entire day's pay? Every driver is constantly faced with these scenarios. The schools must teach you to follow the strict letter of the law. Your trainer may teach you some of the tricks of the trade.

Your trainer often times will have quite a bit of time in at your company so he can also give you priceless insight into how the company is run and who you should get to know. He can give you insight into the maintenance program, dispatching structure, management personnel, equipment the company uses, the company's best traffic lanes, ways to get more home time, how to get more miles, which divisions might suit your particular needs the best, and on and on.

I can't begin to stress how important this can be for a new driver.

Every company in the country will have a whole group of drivers who love the company and a another group who hate it. Often times the drivers are of equal capability and have the same mileage and home time goals in mind but the difference may be as simple as which dispatcher you have or which division you are in.

I'm going to go into these issues more a little bit later but for now let me suggest that you tell your trainer exactly what your goals and expectations are for things like mileage, regions of the country you would like to run, and home time. He can surely help lead you to the right people and the right divisions.

If you're working for a rather small company you simply may not have much of a choice. So to get the most out of your training period don't just ask your trainer tips about driving but also get all the insight into the company that you can get. These insights will be a major factor in the success you will have or lack thereof at your first company.

You're On Your Own Now

Well at this point you've paid your money, made it through the schooling, got hired at your first company, and completed the initial training period. You've made it to the big time..you're on your own. Well, let's put it a better way.... you have your own truck.

But if you're with a good company you are never on your own...there is always someone there to help you when you need it. We're going to get into the specifics of dealing with the people in your own company and also dealing with the customers you are serving later on.

For now let's start with the basics of everyday life on the road...eating, sleeping, showering, parking, shopping, etc. The basics. This part of the job is the simplest part to handle. Let's start out with an introduction to truck stops.

Truck stops will range in size from nothing but a gas station with a gravel lot big enough to park one truck out back to behemoth palaces that are basically a small city within themselves. Finding a place to park can be by far one of the most difficult and frustrating aspects of driving.

The truck stops fill up in the evening and most places with large parking lots like grocery stores and malls don't want you there. So anyplace with truck parking, a bathroom, and something to eat and drink is a blessing no matter how small the place is.

The quality of food at the larger truck stop chains has gotten really good over the years. Many of them have excellent seafood, steaks, chicken, and pastas. One recent trend is for truck stops to put in fast food places also.

It makes perfect sense because sometimes you just want to grab something quick to keep rolling and sometimes you want to sit down for a nice meal. The truck stop makes money by renting out the space to the fast food place so everybody wins. You won't hear me complaining.

Many times I've come off the road and had people say, "boy, I bet you can't wait to get a good home-cooked meal." Of course I don't tell them otherwise but I think you'll be surprised at how good the food is at a lot of truck stops. But unfortunately it's not cheap.

Not even close.

A nice steak dinner with vegetables, bread, and a trip to the salad bar will cost you like $15 or so. You can get a slightly less pricey meal but expect any good meal, breakfast, lunch, or dinner, to run you an average of $12 after tip.

Showers are free if you get fuel at that truck stop. You'll want to shower at the bigger truck stops though because the smaller ones either won't have showers or they tend to be a bit on the dirty side sometimes. The larger truck stops have very nice, very CLEAN individual shower rooms.

You won't have any problems with 'em. The truck stop will supply the towels and soap. All you need is a change of clothing and you're good to go.

Now procedures for fueling will vary greatly from company to company, and sometimes even from division to division within a company. For starters, you NEVER pay for fuel unless you own your own truck, which I desperately hope you won't attempt until you have some years under your belt.

Actually I hope you never attempt it, but that's a debate for another time.

Your company will give you a fuel card which basically acts like a credit card. Some companies will let you fuel anywhere you want but most will have a list of approved fuel stops because they will negotiate better prices with certain truck stops. You will usually be able to buy some supplies for the truck with this card like oil and washer fluid also. That will be about it though.

The company card is not actually a credit card and will not work for purchases other than fuel and supplies at certain truck stops. But finding places for you to go to for fuel, a shower, and something to eat will be quite simple for you to figure out.

There are several books published which sell at most truck stops that will list most of the truck stops in the country in order either by interstate highway or by state.

So wherever you are you can just look in the book and it will tell you where all of the truck stops are on your route, how big they are, and what services they provide like 24 hour restaurant, 24 hour repair shop, check cashing, showers, etc.

By the time you are done with your training period your trainer will have shown you how to handle these everyday aspects of the road. It will be little or no concern to you by the time you are out on your own.

As far as sleeping goes the beds in these trucks nowadays are quite comfortable. Most companies have trucks with sleepers you can stand up in and many of them even have bunk beds. I like to sleep on the bottom bunk and use the upper bunk for storage.

That's what most drivers do.

You will sleep with the truck running when the weather requires it and the thermostat control will be right next to your head.

You can reach up and change it without even getting out from under the covers which is REALLY nice if you accidentally fall asleep without turning the heat on in the winter time and wake up and find you can see your breath (you think I'm kidding...it WILL happen to you I promise).

Sleeping with the truck running is no problem either. You will get used to it real quick. One time I took my mom on a short overnight trip with me from Orlando to Miami. We arrived in Miami around 10 P.M. and had to deliver the next morning. She had never been in a truck before that day.

I told her she would sleep on the top bunk. She mentioned being a bit concerned about how well she would sleep with the truck running but five seconds after her head hit the pillow she was out cold. She didn't wake up once during the night and woke up the next morning feeling great.

So if sleeping with the truck running doesn't bother my ma, well, you should be able to handle it too.

Getting repairs done is similar to getting fuel. Many of the big truck truck stops will have repair shops on the property. Otherwise there is usually one close by. The larger trucking companies will often times have accounts set up with certain repair shops so getting work done is simply a matter of having the truck stop call your company to get the repairs done.

Once they are finished you sign the paperwork and you're out of there. Simple as that. If you are are a shop without a company account set up your company will issue an authorization number over the phone which the repair shop can turn in to get paid. Either way it's usually a pretty simple process that should never involve any money out of your pocket.

Towing works the same way. Your company will find a tow truck for you based on your location and pay for it. If you will need repairs done that will take more than one day, which unfortunately is pretty common, your company will pay for a hotel for you.

So as you can see the everyday issues like food, fuel, repairs, and parking are really quite simple and convenient for the driver to handle most of the time.

If you work for a large company with a lot of accounts set up nationwide and a special division within the company that handles things like finding repair shops and tow trucks for you then life will be much easier on you as a driver.

On My Own For The First Time

So I made it to the big time! I'm going out on my own in my own truck for the first time. 21 years old and driving an 80,000 pound rig coast to coast for a living. It's nearly impossible to describe how excited I was!

I knew there would be a lot of tough times ahead but I was very confident that I would be able to figure them out. Well, I'm still here alive and well so obviously I made it through.

But HOLY CRAP did I have some moments!

DAMN!

Surprisingly enough I don't remember my first trip. Really at this point you would think, “well, why the hell doesn't he just make something up? I want to hear about some disasters!” Don't worry, I have some truly unbelievable stories! But my first trip must have went ok or I would surely remember it.

One of my first memories was of a trip to New York City. Now NYC is the most horrific place to take a big rig anywhere in the country. To me it was AT LEAST ten times worse than the second worse place to take a big rig, which I'd say is Los Angeles or Chicago.

To be honest, throughout my career I DESPISED going to NYC but there really wasn't any other city I didn't want to go to. Chicago, Atlanta, Los Angeles, St Louis, Miami...it didn't matter. I really didn't mind any of them. Just NYC.

To me, and to most drivers for that matter, NYC really is that bad.

As you might expect, one of my most horrendous ordeals was early in my career in NYC. Now you might be wondering why they would send a new driver to the most dangerous and difficult place in the U.S.?

For a very good reason actually – they're idiots.

Total morons.

Rejects that have never been in a truck and don't have any idea what they are getting you into.

All they know is that everybody hates going to NYC and since you're the new guy it's easier to convince you that you have no choice. Also, they figure it's a good test to see what you're made of as a driver.

Again, this is why dispatchers generally hide behind bullet-proof glass.

Total morons.

I call to get directions to my delivery and make my first discovery about NYC...most people have no idea how to get around that city.

How can that be?

Because a huge portion of the population uses public transportation.

They don't even own a vehicle.

The streets are so overcrowded and there is such a shortage of parking that you would have to be crazy to try to try driving yourself around. Cabs, subways, and buses are far faster, cheaper, and easier to take than your own car.

It's quite common to find people in the city that don't have a driver's license and have never owned a vehicle. Think I'm kidding? Not at all.

It took like three different people before I found one that could give me directions to their place. Of course none of them spoke English as their primary language so it took a while to understand what he was saying. But eventually I had my directions and I was on my way.

You have to remember that at the time there were no GPS units and the trucker's atlas wasn't detailed enough to get you where you needed to go. I stopped and bought a detailed folding map of the city which later came in handy, but nothing could have prepared me for the mess I was about to get myself into.

I had two deliveries to make in Queens. How lucky. Pffff.... I remember I came into the city from the west across the George Washington Bridge. At the time there was a huge sign almost immediately after you crossed into the Bronx that read, "Low clearance ahead – all trucks must take next exit".

Ok perfect – I was a nervous wreck to begin with and now ten seconds after crossing into NYC I was faced with a totally unexpected situation. I didn't even have time to ask what the deal was on the CB. The next exit came up and I took it....

......straight into the dead center of the Bronx.

I got to the stop light at the end of the ramp and there wasn't a single sign explaining what the hell I should do now. I looked above at the expressway going overhead that I had just exited from and saw truck after truck continuing on. I was the only one that had gotten off at the exit.

WHAT THE HELL?

Ok, I figured the sign was old and should have been removed and I was the only one that didn't know that at the time. So I'll just get back on the expressway and continue on, right? Wrong.

There was no on ramp to get back on. I was going to have to find my way around the Bronx and get back on track toward Queens. I was nearly certain I was going to throw up.

This could NOT be happening.

I wandered a bit and can't remember what road I was on but it was a four lane highway and I came to my next realization about New York...SOME of the bridges are marked a foot lower than they really are.

Apparently it's to compensate for the snow and ice that may build up under the bridge in the winter. Problem was some bridges were marked with their real height, some were marked a foot shorter than they really are, and there was no way to tell which was which.

My truck was 13' 6" and I came down an incline to a bridge marked 12' 6". I stopped short of the bridge. I decided I would be safer if I went around it on a service road but would have to back up to get there.

So here I am going backwards up the hill as cars are flying by me on both sides. Nothing left in my stomach to throw up so I had to settle for the dry heaves. I get up the hill and get around the bridge and continue on.

After a number of wrong turns and close calls I make it to my deliveries. I want to kill myself. I'm told by my company I have to pick up a load of air freight from JFK airport, which isn't too far away, and head out of the city with it.

I make it to JFK alright and while I'm getting loaded another truck from my company pulls up to load next to me. It was a team of two guys that were both brand new drivers (dispatch at this company were idiots...total morons). I had a couple months experience, they had a couple weeks. They, too, had barf stains on their shirts.

We shared our nightmare stories and looked at our atlases to figure out how to get back out of the city. We had to head west and realized that our luck had finally changed and our nightmare was about to end. We had a straight shot out of the city on the Belt Parkway! Oh thank GOD this ordeal was soon going to be over!

We got our loads and headed to the parkway. It was winter time so it was already dark outside about 6 p.m. Traffic was moving ok but it was insanely busy! Our first clue that something was wrong came when we realized that we were the only trucks on this expressway. Seemed odd but who cares...we just wanted to get out of there.

Second clue that something was wrong came when we realized how low some of the bridges were. At about the third bridge we went under the other driver behind me said he had seen a few sparks come off the top of my trailer as I went under. Oh my god that was close but it was ok. Right after that traffic came to a halt. Rush hour.

The final clue that something was wrong came when I realized the guy in the car next to me was leaning his head out the window trying to get my attention.

I was hoping he was going to tell me what a great job he thought I was doing...and how cool he thought truck drivers were....

......but even though he MAY have been thinking that, it wasn't exactly word for word what he said.

What he actually said was, "This is a parkway and you don't belong here! This isn't for trucks! You're not going to make it under the next bridge, it's too low!"

So naturally I said what anyone would have said in my position –

"WHAT?!?".

"It's too low for you to go under!," he said.

PARKWAY?!?!?!?

Oh my God I just remembered what they told us in school....my next realization about NYC....parkways are for cars only. Trucks are not allowed there!

Oh my God.

This day was truly the worst day of my trucking life!

So here we were...stuck. Couldn't get under the next bridge. Oh my God. Just then I looked in the mirror and saw a couple of trucks with yellow flashing lights coming up behind us. Maybe this was our break. They pulled up on the shoulder next to us and said they'd help us out. They would block traffic to allow us to get to the shoulder.

They did and then they proposed the craziest idea I had ever heard.

They pointed to a roadway that was about one hundred yards across a field and up a slight incline. The guy said, "get a rolling start on the shoulder and then turn across the field. The ground is frozen and should hold. We'll go up on that highway and block traffic. You come across the field onto the highway and follow it to the expressway you belong on. It'll take you back across the George Washington Bridge and out of the city."

Oh my God.

You've gotta be mother-truckin kidding me!

But alas, we clearly had no choice. So in the utter darkness we were going to take loaded big rigs across the frozen field (there was only a dusting of snow on the ground), up the incline, and onto the roadway which will eventually lead to a safe way out of the city.

Ok, sure. Hell, what could go wrong? Oh my God. So we saw traffic clear on the highway we were destined for. We got a rolling start, grabbed all the gears we could get, kept our foot on the floor, and there we went – two rigs across the field, up the incline, and bounced over the curb onto the empty highway.

Holy crap we did it!!!

Looking back in the mirror we saw that thousands of people were sitting at a standstill behind us waiting to be released so they could continue their commute home. We kept our foot on the floor and headed toward the George Washington Bridge as fast as we could.

When we made it to the bridge, the gateway out of the city, it was a rush I don't think I had ever felt before! Everything that could possibly have gone wrong that day did...except one thing...we didn't hit anything!

Yeah, I scraped the bridge, but shut up!!!

I'm not talking about that!

I mean no fender benders, no running over cars, nothing. I got dumped into the middle of the Bronx with no idea what to do, got lost numerous times, backed up up a hill going the wrong way to get out from under a bridge, made several u-turns, illegally got onto a parkway, held up thousands of commuters trying to get home, drove a loaded big rig across a frozen field on a cold winter's night, and nearly threw up on myself several dozen times!

But regardless, we did it!

We made it out unscathed!!!! I was screaming WOO HOO at the top of my lungs!!!!! I looked out over Manhattan from the top of that Bridge and realized I had escaped the most horrible nightmare of my truckin life! Oh my God we made it out alive! Insane.

NYC is truly a nightmare in a big rig. I love going to Manhattan for vacations and holidays but I fly in and take cabs everywhere. It's a ton of fun. But driving a truck around that city is a nightmare. I don't know how anybody could see it any other way.

So I worked at that company a few more months and then came another memorable experience. I was driving through Arkansas one night and went through a weigh station. They told me to pull around back and two officers came out to greet me.

They looked at my logbook, which was fine, and presumably because I was quite young and had very long hair they thought I might have something on me that I shouldn't have and asked me if they could search my vehicle. I told them they could and they did.

I was standing outside the truck talking to another officer when the one inside the truck popped his head out the window and held up a small object and said, “what's this?”

Uh oh. It appeared to be a small pipe...kind of like a pipe you might smoke marijuana from I'd say.

Well, they would say so too.

Now they were really gonna look hard for drugs. I knew I didn't have any and in fact the pipe was in an old jacket that I had totally forgotten about.

Bad, bad luck for me.

Well, a few minutes later the officer searching the truck called me and the other officer over. He showed us a small wrapper of tinfoil and said to me, “what do we have here?" Well, I knew exactly what it was and said, "oh my god" and looked down at the ground.

The searching officer sat in the driver's seat, his partner sat in the passenger seat, and they told me to sit in the sleeper. I had a cooler in between the seats and the searching officer carefully placed the small tinfoil wrapper on the cooler, and all three of us leaned our heads over the top of it as he slowly began to peel open the wrapper.

Slowly, carefully he pulled it open and just as he got the last of it peeled open to reveal what was in the middle.

I took in a long, deep gasp and from about a foot away I looked the searching officer in the eye and proclaimed, "A Hershey's Kiss!!!!!"

....and indeed it was.

Earlier that day I had eaten one and had thrown the wrapper in the garbage. I had known it all along but couldn't resist playing along like they had caught me with drugs.

Holy SH#T were they mad!

Turns out they didn't think that was funny at all! Who knew???? Turns out that's not the first time I found something funnier than the person I was teasing had found it.

But you'll have that sometimes.

Well, they actually wrote me a ticket for having the pipe and let me go. Seems they should have arrested me or something but for whatever reason they didn't.

Well, about a week later I had returned home and my company called to inform me I was fired. Not the start to my dream career I was looking for. It appears that company never put that information out for any other companies to see because the subject never came up again.

Huh, go figure.

So I was sitting in Atlanta one day without a job and decided it was time for a change. I loved NASCAR and so decided I'd try moving to Charlotte, NC and see what that was like. So I packed everything I owned into my duffel bag, threw it in my old truck, and took off.

I arrived in Charlotte and on my first day I interviewed for a job with a local company that was based there. They told me I had to take two written tests...one was a safety test, the other a "personality" test to see if I was the type of person they were looking for.

The personality test was very odd. It was multiple choice and filled with very odd questions like, "Which of the following best describes you?". The four choices were horrible things, something like lazy, sloppy, careless, and selfish.

Oh, ok.

So I picked one.

The next question would be something like, “Which of the following least describes you?,” and had choices like hard-working, diligent, organized, and giving. Oh, ok. So I picked one. The whole test was like that!

Well, they told me I aced the safety test but failed the personality test so they couldn't hire me but thanked me for my time.

I have a great personality and if those rotten, idiotic, brain-dead bastards couldn't see that then they could burn in hell. They wouldn't know a nice guy if their cross-eyed, toothless, fat-nosed faces were looking straight at one!

MORONS! Screw em.

So I went to work for a different company in the area and that's when I learned some incredibly important lessons about dealing with trucking companies, especially the larger ones. You see, this company really wasn't a very good company overall. Their equipment was safe, but old and uncomfortable for the most part. Their freight was mostly short runs and centered around the northeastern part of the US. Their management was totally out of touch with the drivers and clearly didn't understand technology and how the industry was changing both within the offices and from the driver's perspective.

So why did I work there? Well, for one it was easy to get a job there and the terminal was close to where I was living. I didn't really bother doing much research into my options. I was broke and just wanted to get back on the road making money and took the first thing I found.

My experience at the company overall actually turned out to be a great one. Even though the company had mostly old equipment, I managed to get myself into one of the only newer trucks they had. Now THAT really pissed off a lot of other drivers.

I also got a lot of long runs to the west coast even though most solo drivers stayed on the east coast. I made great money, had a nice truck, and got a lot of the runs everybody else was trying unsuccessfully to get.

How did I do it?

I figured out a few key things you have to do in order to make the best of your career at any company.

Hang on to your hat, you're gonna love this.

How To Handle Your Own Company

These next two sections will have the biggest impact on how much money you will make and how happy you will be working for your chosen company. We're gonna start with the issues, people, and systems within your own company and then move on to the customers whose freight you'll be hauling.

No matter what the size of the company you work for you must learn to deal with the people in the offices and you must try to understand as much as you possibly can about the systems they use to find freight, distribute the freight amongst the company's drivers, and how they handle issues like breakdowns, home time, logbooks, tractor assignments, and a whole slew of other items.

I can't possibly stress this to you enough....the vast majority of the time you find a driver that is unhappy or unsuccessful with a company it's because they don't understand the office structure, procedures, and key people within their own company.

I've seen this a million times and it's a shame for both the driver and the company because often times both the company and the driver are top notch but they simply don't understand one another's systems and expectations.

I'm gonna help you discover how your company is structured, who has the authority over different types of decisions, and how to get in touch with the right people at the right times. Most of all this section will help you to understand "the rules of the game" within your own company and how to make the system work for you, not against you.

Read on....you're gonna love this.

When it comes to a driver's success throughout his or her career there will always be one factor that will stand out time and time again above all else...more important than the equipment you drive, more important than the freight you haul, and even more important than the company you were working for.

The biggest factor in the level of success and happiness a driver will find will without a doubt be your dispatcher.

Everything begins and ends right here....with dispatch.

Depending on who you ask, dispatchers can go by many names. If you ask someone in middle management in a large company they may call them fleet managers, distribution specialists, driver managers, and other wonderful titles.

They'll smile and say how these people are the backbone of the company and their knowledge, dedication, expertise, and heartfelt appreciation for the hard work their drivers put in has made their company grow into the industry leader it is today.

If you ask experienced drivers about their dispatchers they may agree wholeheartedly with the middle manager's view. Or they may describe them more along the lines of being the most, "idiotic son of a @&%(# I ever knew. That $&^@ is so %*#& $&^@ stupid I'd like to shove his $&$*@ in a $&@*# volcano!"

I can't tell you how many times I've met up with drivers on the road that had the same dispatcher that I had and we had completely opposite opinions of that person.

Maybe I was getting 3200 miles per week and home every weekend while the other person was getting 1800 miles per week and only allowed to go home every other weekend.

Nobody will have more of an influence on your success as a driver than your dispatcher. He or she can be your best friend, worst enemy, or anything in between, sometimes all in the same DAY!!! Of course I can be that way too and without a doubt there have been a number of times I've brought that upon myself.

But hey, I'm not on trial here so get off my back!!

No, seriously though you will find out that you control your own destiny to a very large extent. Pretty soon I'll show you how.

For now, let's start with what exactly your dispatcher does. A dispatcher's duties will vary greatly from company to company. In a smaller company a dispatcher will have a lot more control and authority than in a larger company, generally speaking of course.

First and foremost though your dispatcher will be the number one day to day contact point you will have with your company. Almost every single time you call or message your company it will be directed to your dispatcher.

You will deal directly with each other one on one but you will not be the only driver your dispatcher will be handling. He or she will have anywhere from 5 to 60 different drivers on their "board". A dispatcher's board is simply the group of drivers he/she is handling at any given time.

If someone else's dispatcher calls in sick you may find that your dispatcher will have to cover his or her board that day and it will likely take you longer to get replies to your messages.

Your dispatcher's first duty is to exchange information with you. All of your load information will be given to you by your dispatcher. Any questions, problems, or concerns you have will be directed back to him or her. Basically all of your normal, everyday communication with your company will be with dispatch.

At times you will need someone with more authority or you may have an issue with you dispatcher personally and you need to talk with someone higher up. We'll cover those things in a little while.

Dispatchers usually have the lowest level of authority within the company's office. Some dispatchers will also handle the "load planning" which means deciding which drivers get which loads each day. Often times in smaller companies the dispatcher will have this authority. In larger companies they may or may not.

Often times a larger company will have a dedicated group of people, we'll call them "load planners" that decide which drivers get which loads but the information is actually given to the driver by the dispatcher, not the load planner. I have worked within both systems and always found that the more authority my dispatcher had the better things went for me.

Here's why:

Since you deal with your dispatcher directly day in and day out, nobody in your company knows you better. Your dispatcher knows how many miles you like to get each week, what areas of the country you like to run, how hard working and reliable you are, how flexible you are, whether or not you'll cheat on your logbook, how often you like to be home, what types of loads and how many miles you've been getting lately, and so on.

If there is a load planner distributing the loads, that load planner likely doesn't know you or much of anything about you. Just like a dispatcher will have a group of drivers on his or her board, a load planner will likely have either a region of the country or a group of several different dispatchers that he or she is responsible for handling.

I'll give you an example of how this can work:

Say you are running regional and getting home every weekend. You like at least 2500 miles per week, you work hard, you're reliable, you've been with the company for five years, and you have a wife and three kids at home. On Monday load planner A gives you a 300 mile load from New Jersey to Pennsylvania for Tuesday. Now, on Tuesday you're in load planner B's region and you get a 200 mile run from western PA to Baltimore, MD for Wednesday delivery.

Now, on Wednesday you are in load planner C's region and you get a 180 mile run back into New Jersey. If you normally shoot for 2500 miles per week and you're running 5 days and home weekends, then you're averaging about 500 miles per day normally.

Well, here you are on sitting back in New Jersey on Thursday morning with only 680 miserable miles and you're supposed to be home in another day or two. There is no chance whatsoever you're going to have a good week this week. You may only get half the miles you were hoping for.

Why did this happen?

Why didn't you're dispatcher do anything about it?

See, in this type of system the dispatcher has less authority than the load planners. If a load planner says, “this is the way it is” then that's the way it is. Your dispatcher can not overrule the load planner. Now a good dispatcher who really cares about their drivers will beg and plead with the load planners to get you the best freight possible.

The office in this type of system is in a constant state of lobbying. Deals are being made and compromises being sought day and night. But the problem is that the load planners often times don't really care. It's not THEIR drivers who are unhappy, it's the dispatcher's drivers. Besides, their job is to move the freight efficiently within their region, not to move it in a way that makes every driver happy.

Once they move a particular driver out of their region it's not their problem anymore.

Believe me I'm not making this stuff up. I've lived it. There's a reason that most companies have locks on the doors and bullet proof glass separating the drivers from the dispatchers and load planners. You think I'm kidding? I'm not.

One time I went to work for a company that three months prior had a driver pull into the terminal, walk into the dispatcher's office, and shoot his dispatcher in the back of the head. Dead. The driver walked back out, sat in his truck, and waited for the police to come get him.

Life in prison.

Every word of it is true.

When I say your dispatcher can make you mad sometimes, I mean REALLY mad sometimes. No joke.

But a system that adds a layer of load planning above your dispatcher can be very difficult to deal with. The key is to find a system where everyone's interests are the same. If your dispatcher has the authority to do your load planning and your dispatcher is eligible for bonuses based on the number of miles and the level of service his or her drivers are providing then you and your dispatcher both benefit when you are getting a lot of miles.

This is a great scenario.

So many times a driver will just automatically blame the dispatcher when things are not going his way. One of the first things you should find out when you are interviewing for a job with a company is who is responsible for what. That way if you aren't getting home on time or you're not getting the miles you were hoping for you will know who is to blame.

I can't tell you how many times I've talked to drivers that kept switching dispatchers and weren't getting anywhere because they didn't know the system for one, and for two they didn't know the chain of command so when things weren't going well they didn't even know who to talk to about it. Many times an impatient driver won't even bother to figure out what the problem is....he just quits and says the company sucks.

You have to understand the command chain and who has responsibility for what.

Now no matter how much authority your dispatcher may or may not have, and no matter how good of a company you work for, if you get stuck with a dispatcher who simply doesn't care about his or her drivers your life is going to be miserable a good portion of the time.

Fortunately most dispatchers do care to some extent about you as a driver.

Also if you have a dispatcher who doesn't get along well with the other people in the office, especially load planners and higher up managers like operations managers and terminal managers, you may not get the miles and home time you would otherwise be getting on the board of a more friendly dispatcher.

This is especially true if your dispatcher must depend on other people to assign loads. If you think the load planners would understand that a group of drivers shouldn't be punished because their dispatcher is a jerk, well, sometimes they don't really think about it that way.

They may figure, “hey, dispatcher A is a jerk and dispatcher B is really sweet so I HATE doing favors for A. I like giving the good loads to B. She's always so sweet.” Sure it effects the lives of the drivers far more than that of the dispatchers and load planners, but most of the people that work in the offices of trucking companies were never actually drivers, so they don't really understand the implications of their actions too well.

Now another HUGE problem I've seen drivers bring upon themselves is having the attitude that, "hey, if this company wants me to run the lousy loads then they better give me some good ones first." I have seen tons and tons of drivers that have taken the attitude that the company has to prove itself to them before they are going to go out of their way for the company.

If you are going to take this approach then let me help you out here....just take a trip to NYC, go to the top of the Empire State Building, then jump off the building and land squarely on your face. Believe me you will save yourself and others a lot of suffering.

Ask yourself this, "why would a company go out of their way to make life easy on a brand new driver by giving him or her great loads all of the time?" Haven't they spent a ton of time and money on you already?

Haven't they already paid for your physical, transported you to the terminal, put you through orientation, given you a beautiful truck to drive, agreed to a nice pay package for you which likely includes great benefits, 401k, and direct deposit, and incurred the liability risks of having you as an employee?

Now make a list of all of the things you've done for them.

Hmmmm.....awfully short list isn't it? They have done all of this for you based solely on the POTENTIAL for you to be a good driver. Now why don't you fulfill your end of the bargain and SHOW them what you're capable of? Show them that you are worthy of all of the time, money, and risk.

There is a simple cliché we've all heard....give and ye shall receive. Try it. You'll be amazed.

Your company likely has tons of proven drivers, dispatchers, mechanics, salespeople, and managers that have actually made money for the company and done a great job over a long period of time. They are the bedrock of the company.

After all your company has already done for you without you having done anything for them, what would you expect them to do now.....give you all of the good loads and make their proven veterans suffer with all of the lousy ones?

Let you make a ton of money while the drivers that have become the foundation of the company make very little?

Now that I've laid this all out for you and given you this perspective on things it should be painfully obvious to you that you should come into a new company with the attitude that you're going to work hard, be safe, pick up and deliver on time, and just be the best driver you are capable of being so that someday soon you can call your dispatcher and request a few more miles and a mix of better runs each week in return for the great job you've done proving yourself to be a valuable commodity for the company. It SHOULD be painfully obvious anyway.

But for some reason the industry is rampant with brand new drivers that somehow feel everybody still owes them something for nothing. I'm honestly not sure where this thought process is coming from, but I hope it won't continue with you.

Make sure you take the time to discuss your goals and expectations with your dispatcher early and often in your career at the company. First of all you may have false expectations based on lies you've been told or misconceptions you may have had regarding your company or the industry in general.

I've found a lot of new drivers are under the impression that when a company says you'll get about 2200 miles per week and home on weekends that it's going to be that way every single week.

It's not. I'll tell you that right now.

The industry is cyclical and inconsistent by nature. Expect it. You may AVERAGE 2200 miles per week and home on weekends but it WILL NOT happen that way every week. Some weeks may be double the miles and half the home time, other weeks may be the other way around. Go with the flow. That's just the way it is.

Now I want you to take a balanced approach to this issue so be aware of something...there are some dispatchers that will take advantage of a driver who doesn't know what they should expect in terms of mileage, home time, and the type of loads they will be getting.

On many occasions I have talked with drivers who were being given half the miles and home time they should have been getting and on top of that, they were repeatedly being given the most difficult loads to the most difficult places. It's a shame, but that's people for ya. You will always find a rotten apple in a bunch.

Again I stress this to you...discuss the expectations with your company and especially with your dispatcher:

What is the average length of the loads in your company or your division?

How often can you expect to be home?

Where will you be expected to run?

Can you expect to be home on the holidays?

Will you have to help load or unload trucks?

If so, how often and what does it pay?

Your trainer can definitely help you out a lot with many of these expectations so don't miss out on the chance to learn all you can during your training period.

Now let's assume that you got a job with what seems to be a great company. You went through your training period and have been assigned your own truck. You were assigned a dispatcher, met with this person, and had the chance to discuss the expectations you have of each other. You head out with the key to your truck in your hand and you're as excited as you can be.

But a month later you've found that you're not getting the miles you expected, you're not getting home as much as you expected, and no matter how many conversations

you have had with your dispatcher about it nothing seems to change. What do you do? There's a number of things you should do. Shooting your dispatcher in the head is definitely NOT one of them though! (...and I MEAN THAT!...) Let's take a look...

The first thing I always did was to simply ask my dispatcher if freight is slow right now. After proving myself to be a good driver who was reliable, safe, and anxious to get good miles it was rare to find myself getting lousy miles when most of the other drivers were doing well.

If I had a good dispatcher and the miles were available, I was getting my share. So usually if I wasn't rolling strong, either were most of the other trucks. However I wasn't one to sit back and lose money without investigating further. So the next step for me was to start talking to other drivers.

Look around in the truck stops and on the highways for other drivers at your company. Simply ask em straight out, "hey, have you been getting good miles lately? I've been slow the last couple weeks." If they've been slow also, then maybe things are just slow right now. That used to happen quite a bit. If they've been busy then I used to wonder, "if he's getting the miles, why ain't I?"

Find out what division that driver is in and who their dispatcher is. Getting their truck number will help more than anything though.

Do this with at least 3 drivers in order to look for some kind of pattern. I'd say 90% of the time if I wasn't getting the miles most of the other drivers weren't either. However if several other drivers tell you things are going well for them then it's time to call dispatch again. The more information you can give your dispatcher the better. Don't just say, "hey, everyone is runnin, why ain't I?"

Remember, your dispatcher is usually on your side and sometimes doesn't have the authority to assign loads. So maybe your dispatcher is under the impression that things are slow but in reality there is something else going on in the office somewhere.

So if you can say, "hey I talked to truck numbers 22, 46, and 98 and they all said they are getting good miles" then now you know you have presented your dispatcher with solid facts that he or she can use to start their own investigation. This puts you as a driver in a great position.

You know other people are getting the miles but you aren't. If you have been lobbying for more miles and have been doing a good job then you know something is wrong somewhere. You've presented the facts to your dispatcher so now he or she knows that YOU know that something is wrong.

This will give you good insight into the quality of your dispatcher. He or she should now present this information to their boss and to the load planners and get the situation resolved.

In larger companies there will be times when by the luck of the draw a driver will accidentally get overlooked. You may have had a slow week or two but it's an honest mistake on their part. Nobody was out to get you and the company doesn't suck, it was just an oversight. In this case you should find that your dispatcher will come back to you and say, "hey, I've gotten it taken care of".

They didn't realize what was going on and now they do so they're going to send some good loads your way. Sorry bout that." Problem solved. This scenario is happening to somebody, somewhere everyday at the larger companies. If you take the time to talk things over you'll find that situations like this come and go all the time and are soon forgotten.

Nothing to it. No harm done.

You'll get your lost miles back in the coming week or two.

Be patient.

However, let's explore other possibilities. Say you've presented this information to your dispatcher complete with truck numbers and everything. You ask dispatch to please look into it and see if you can get more miles. They agree to do so and come back to you later saying they talked to their boss and the problem is solved. But several days or a week go by and still nothing gets better.

Ok, now on to the next step...your dispatcher's boss.

Ask your dispatcher for the name and extension of their boss. But make it clear that you're not calling to complain about them but to see if you can find out why you still aren't getting any miles. You'll find that your dispatcher's boss has several dispatchers under him or her.

So have an honest discussion with the boss and make it clear that you're looking to get more miles and you've presented your dispatcher with the truck numbers of other drivers that are getting good miles. Continue to explain that you asked your dispatcher to look into it and you were told it was taken care of and yet nothing has changed.

At this point you will get some insight into the current freight situation within the company and some insight into your dispatcher. Explain to the boss that you need the miles and you're not looking to get anybody into trouble or anything but if the miles are available and you aren't getting them then maybe you aren't with the dispatcher that's right for you.

Ask about the reputation of your dispatcher:

Is he or she known as the type who keeps their drivers running?

Are they the type that really cares about their drivers?

Even though the dispatcher doesn't have the authority to overrule the load planners they are responsible for making everyone aware of a driver that is not being taken care of properly. If your dispatcher isn't letting anyone know that you're not happy then they aren't doing their job.

Keep in mind that your dispatcher and their boss work together everyday. They know each other well and will often defend, or at least try not to offend each other. So the boss might say, "hey, your dispatcher is a good one and we'll keep an eye out to make sure you start getting some good loads." At this point you should give it another few days or a week and see if anything changes.

What if nothing changes? On to the next boss. Don't scream and yell. Don't threaten anyone. Be civil and be patient. Explain yourself and your situation thoroughly and if you're a good driver you'll likely soon find the problem and get it resolved. But understand something...if you are the type of driver that won't drive at night, you don't like the northcast, you're afraid of the snow, the glare from the rain bothers you, and so on and so on, then let me take the mystery out of your situation for you....you aren't getting the miles because you don't WANT the miles.

Here's some more plain truth for ya....trucking is a very tough job that takes a tremendous amount of dedication, determination, and long, hard hours of work. If you aren't willing to put in the effort and stick it out when things get tough, then the drivers who do will be getting all the miles. Unfortunately this is another common scenario related to a driver's expectations.

Driving, especially over the road and regional jobs, are definitely NOT 9 to 5 kind of jobs. They require an unbelievable amount of flexibility and dedication. Your job is to get the freight picked up and delivered on time, safely. The more miles you run the more money you make AND the more money the company makes. S

o if you won't run at night, in the wind, in the snow, on Thursdays, on partly cloudy days, wet roads, or on days when you don't feel like it well then I ask you, “HOW ARE YOU GONNA GET ANY WORK DONE????”

Generally speaking, if you won't do it then somebody else will. The load planners and dispatchers are responsible for getting the freight moved. If they have ten guys that run their butts off and ten lazy ones, then the ten hard workers are going to be very well taken care of. The ten lazy ones? Nobody is going to be too concerned with them. It all boils down to who is getting the job done.

Here's a scenario I've had happen to me about five hundred times: I'm walking into a truck stop and a driver asks me if I've been getting a lot of miles. At the time I was and so I tell em, “oh yeah I've been getting a ton” and they say, “geez, I don't get crap!” Well, I'll try to figure out why. I'll ask who their dispatcher is, what division they're in, how long they've been at the company, and how many miles they usually get.

At this point they spill their guts. 95% of the time they'll start telling stories about different loads they've been running and slowly but surely the truth comes out....they don't WANT the miles. Maybe they THINK they're a good driver and they just don't realize that they aren't getting the job done as well as they should be. They won't run hard enough, they complain about every other load for one reason or another, they're late half the time, and for one reason or another they just aren't getting it done.

Now sometimes this isn't true. Sometimes they may just have the wrong dispatcher, or they're in a slow division, or they're being accidentally overlooked. But generally speaking there is a rule you can go by....if you're not getting the miles then there's a reason for it. Maybe they aren't available, maybe you're in a slow division, maybe you're with the wrong dispatcher, OR maybe you just STINK as a driver!

However, let me present you with one more possibility (I'm loading my gun here....getting ready to fire a HUGE blast here in a moment...). What if you're running in all types of weather, during the day or at night, not complaining about the loads you're getting, and all in all you can't figure out why you aren't getting the miles you were hoping for?

Well, maybe you've noticed that every time you turn around you seem to be running out of hours on your logbook.

It seems several times per week you have to shut down a couple hours short of the customer and have to reschedule your load. Then you sit for a day or two afterwards. You talk to drivers that are turning 2800 miles per week but you can't figure out how to get more than like 1800 miles without running out of hours sometimes. What's the deal here?

A lot of times drivers in this position would admit that it seems every time they have to shut down because they're out of hours their dispatcher seems annoyed. It's not the driver's fault he or she is out of hours, that's just the way the laws are written and yet it seems the driver gets punished for it by sitting a day or two afterwards.

As a driver you can't PROVE they are punishing you, and nobody is actually saying you did anything wrong, but the pattern and the attitude your seeing sure suggests it.

Well, the reason I'm writing this book is to explain the raw truth about the trucking industry.

I'm not worried about what anybody will think about what I'm saying here. I'm just letting you know what to expect and clue you in to the REALITIES of life as a truck driver. I'm going to come back later on in this book to helping you deal with more of the people and systems at work within your own company. But first I have to take a long detour here to explain a number of important facts about life in the trucking industry so you will have a deeper understanding of all of the nuances involved with how you handle yourself, your company, and your career as a commercial driver.

So here comes some of the coldest, hardest truths about the industry....it's time to start telling it like it is....so hang on to your seat....you may NOT like this next part.

EVERYBODY WINS WHEN DRIVERS CHEAT THE BOOK

It's true. If the driver cheats on his logbook, everybody benefits. How is that? Simple...drivers get paid by the mile and so do the trucking companies themselves. So the more miles a driver runs in a given amount of time, the more money the driver makes AND the more money the driver's company will make.

As an added bonus, the more miles you are turning per truck and per driver in a given amount of time the more efficiently you are moving goods for your customers overall.

The more efficiently you move goods overall the more efficiently our economy runs as a whole. So as you can clearly see, if one driver can find a way to turn more miles in any given amount of time it benefits the driver, his company, the customers you are serving, and the overall economy as a whole.

That's why governments on every level try to give the impression that they are serious about cracking down on drivers and companies that break the laws and yet in all reality they do very little or nothing about it. If they were to seriously crack down on the abuse they would be crippling our own economy.

That doesn't help anyone.

So if the government cracks down on companies they would be hurting their own economy. If the trucking companies were to crack down on their own drivers they would be hurting their own profits. If the drivers took it upon themselves to stop driving when they ran out of hours they would be hurting their own paychecks.

So who has a vested interest in REALLY enforcing the laws?

NOBODY.

ABSOLUTELY NOBODY!

Here's a couple more factors that play into this same scenario which make it an even WORSE idea to try to enforce limits on the drivers. Our highway system is already seriously over-crowded and there has been a big shortage of truck drivers available to the industry for several decades now.

If you further limited the amount of driving a driver could do it would take even MORE fuel-guzzling trucks clogging the already overcrowded highways and even MORE drivers to drive them which we already have a shortage of to move the same amount of freight we are moving today.

Of course the governments, trucking companies, and drivers are all acutely aware of this situation. So what is the solution? Well, that's the problem...there is no easy solution. So what is being done about it? The government does just enough public enforcement to give the impression that they are working vigilantly to keep the drivers and companies from breaking the laws and endangering the public.

In reality the enforcement is sparse and predictable. Even when a certain state is going to do a three day crackdown they ANNOUNCE it ahead of time so everybody knows!

So even the very few that do get caught cheating just pay a small fine and continue doing what they were doing before....breaking the law and profiting from it. Believe me, everybody makes WAY more money by cheating the system than they lose by getting caught once in a great while.

Everybody.

That's why almost everybody cheats. It makes perfect economic sense from the bottom to the top...the drivers, the trucking companies, the American industries, the American people as a whole, and the local, state, and federal government officials who are all trying their best to get re-elected all benefit when drivers cheat.

Oh, and as an added bonus, where does the money go that gets collected from the fines issued to the drivers and the trucking companies that do get caught cheating every so often? To the town, city, state, and federal governments to use any way they damn well please.

Nice little system isn't it?

As a driver you will have to decide for yourself how you want to handle this situation. Now at this point you may think you already know the answer. Some of you are saying:

“Hey, I'M not breaking the law. I don't care what my company thinks and I damn sure don't care what the government thinks. The law says I can only drive a certain number of hours and that's the way it's gonna be. They can't do anything to me if I shut down when I run out of hours so that's what I'm gonna do. Period. Besides, if I don't cheat then I can't get in trouble and then nobody can touch my license or fine me and take my money!”

Well, yes there are a number of drivers that take this approach and it makes perfect sense on the surface. I respect them for making that choice and sticking with it. Outstanding. But let me explain the situation on a little bit deeper level for you so you'll know the reality of the situation that you'll be faced with.

The D.O.T.

Now the DOT, the Department Of Transportation, is the federal agency responsible for the enforcement of the laws governing the commercial trucking industry. The laws are written and enforced as federal laws but in an odd sort of system, the states are in control of their own DOT law enforcement and are free to write their own laws or increase the standards for the enforcement of the federal laws.

In other words, the states can take a federal law and make it even more strict if they so choose. So some states are far more vigilant than others. Also, like with any other system of laws and law enforcement, the enforcement agency can selectively choose what laws to enforce and when and where they would like to enforce them. They can be as harsh or as lenient as they would like to be.

Now if you're familiar with the way any law enforcement agency works, they try to strike a balance between allowing people their right to life, liberty, and the pursuit of happiness by not invading people's privacy and yet at the same time they must keep a leash on troublemakers and maintain control and awareness of the situation.

Part of being able to maintain control means the law enforcement agency must be able to take control of any individual or entity, like a driver or a corporation, whenever they feel it is in their best interest to do so. It's no different for a parent running their own household. As a parent, you write and enforce the rules. As a child gets older they would like more privacy, their own space. Their room.

Well, how can you give them their privacy yet at the same time control the household and make sure the child isn't going to do harm to themselves or anyone else? Well, in all reality you can't do both at the same time.

So you set commonly accepted privacy rules like knocking on their door before entering and staying out of their room and their stuff when they're not around BUUUUUUUT if you feel it's necessary for the good of the child, the household, or to prevent any kind of harm in general you WILL pull rank and barge into their room and rummage through their stuff anyway. You have to...you're responsible and life just isn't that black and white sometimes.

There are the ideals and then there are the realities.

The DOT works the same way. They would like to be able to leave individual drivers and the companies they work for alone, but the reality is that they are responsible for protecting the drivers, the trucking companies, the general public, and the nation and the economy as a whole.

Sooooooo, since they aren't “allowed” to invade your privacy unless a law has been broken or they have a reasonable suspicion, there are times when they will suspect that a person or entity may intentionally or unintentionally be about to cause harm and they need to isolate the cause of that potential harm before any actual harm has been done.

What am I getting at here?

If you think that the DOT won't be able to touch you as long as your truck appears to be safe, you are minding your own business, and your logbook is legal, you are sadly mistaken.

As a commercial driver you fall under federal regulation. If you ever for a moment believe they can't shut you down and take your license away for no apparent reason then you are tragically idealistic. As a truck driver you will be under the constant scrutiny of not only your own company but your own government.

Your truck is being tracked through the use of numerous networked GPS, Camera, and RFID enabled devices every moment of every day. EZPASS, Pre-Pass, Qualcomm, engine signatures, cameras, x-ray machines, and an untold number of other unknowable devices are being used to monitor everything from your engine conditions to your speed, location, elevation, direction, and are keeping track of everyplace that truck has ever been.

If you think the government conspiracy theorists are crazy then just ignore what I'm telling you and believe it isn't true. I just hope for your sake that you aren't choosing to ignore me because if it WAS true you would be doomed. My troubled friend, for your sake I'd suggest running for the border as fast as you can and BY GOD don't do it in a big rig. But heck, what do I know right? Do it your way.

If you pay close attention to overpasses, light poles, intersections, and weigh stations you will see tons and tons of devices all over the place like antennas, cameras, and many other well-disguised devices as you pass on by.

What are these? Well why don't you tell me?

It's hard to figure out what they are exactly but its not hard to figure out what they're doing...they're watching you. They're watching and tracking all of us. Want an example of how bold they're getting with this stuff? Here's a beauty:

Somebody has decided that a great way to try to detect and prevent drivers from falling asleep is to mount a camera inside the truck that is focused on the driver while he or she is driving. The camera will supposedly be monitoring your eyes and can distinguish between blinking and the beginning of somebody falling asleep. If it deems that you are falling asleep it will sound some type of alarm to alert you.

Sounds beautiful. I'll even bet you it can work.

The technology seems quite possible, even fairly straight-forward. So how do you feel about having a camera trained on you every moment you are driving 24/7/365? Hey, I'm personally not one to go overboard with the privacy vs intrusion debate but are you kidding me? A camera on me ALL OF THE TIME? Thanks but no thanks.

That's just insane. But they're working on it. They're working on a ton of things, believe me.

Here's another example of something already being used at the last company I worked for:

They have a GPS enabled device on the rear of their trailers. The device can be tracked with satellites and remains operable even when the trailer is not hooked to any trailer. This device does several things. First of all it lets the company know 24/7/365 in real time where exactly the trailer is and can be accurate within about 50 feet. It also keeps track in real time of the trailer doors being opened or closed and the trailer being attached to or detached from a tractor.

It gets way better...here's how the company can use it:

Say you tell your company you have trailer 1234 and they assign you a load to pick up at 24 High Street, Bristol, CT at 8:00 a.m. Monday morning. It will deliver at 36 Low Street, Boston, MA at 8 a.m. Tuesday morning. All of this load information is in your company's computer system. They assign your truck and trailer to the load. Now the computer system will use the GPS devices on your tractor and trailer to monitor in real time every step of the way. They know where both your truck and the trailer are. They know when you hook up to the trailer and the computer monitors your progress.

The system knows where you are supposed to be going and when you are supposed to arrive there. If it calculates that you have too far to go for the amount of time you have left to get there it will issue an alert to dispatch letting them know you seem to be running late.

It will track when you arrive at the pickup point, when you opened the trailer doors, whether or not you drop the trailer, when you close the trailer doors, where both the truck and trailer are along the route, when you arrive at the destination, when you open the doors, and when you close them again.

The system will store all of this information permanently in case any of it needs to be known anytime in the future for any reason. You, your truck, your trailer, and everything you do related (or maybe not related to) your job is being tracked in real time and being stored permanently somewhere.

If the tracking system looses the signal from any of the tractors or trailers for some short specified amount of time another alert will be sent to dispatch letting them know the last time and location of the equipment and they can send the police if they like to determine if the equipment has been stolen and the devices deactivated.

For the sane amongst us let me assure you that once you get your CDL and set foot in a commercial truck your days of privacy, or perceived privacy, are long gone. You'll find out how true that is the first time you apply for a job at a large company. I can not prove that they are able to use FBI computers to pull up your personal history but I don't know how they could POSSIBLY find out all the things they able to find out about you otherwise.

I do know that the Department of Homeland Security spends an enormous amount of time, money, and resources tracking the trucking industry. They are convinced that terrorists would like to use trucks to attack our cities and landmarks. I'd have to say that they are probably correct. It makes perfect sense.

So if you are trying to hide in any way from any law enforcement agency you should probably stay far away from the idea of getting your CDL. For the rest of you, come on in.

The point of all of of this is to inform you that no matter how legal and untouchable you may THINK you are by having your truck all shined up and your logbook caught up with hours of driving still available I promise you it's an illusion.

You are only free to roam this country in a big rig as a commercial driver because they are allowing you to do so. You do not have the right as a commercial driver to be left alone no matter how perfect having that right may seem. They can shut you down, search your vehicle, and hold you in custody if they really want to or feel they need to.

Now I'm not saying you're likely to be thrown in prison for life for absolutely no reason. I'm simply saying please don't make the mistake of copping an attitude or making a dumb decision based on the facade that you have some God given rights and nobody can take them away from you.

That may indeed turn out to be a big mistake someday.

Punishment: You Can Break The Law, But Not TOO Much

Now I had mentioned just a little while ago the idea that governments are putting up the facade that they are diligently enforcing the laws to protect the American people from drivers and companies that are breaking these laws...especially those laws that pertain to the number of hours a driver can legally drive in any given period of time.

This enforcement is like walking a tight rope because if the news begins reporting that a growing number of drivers are falling asleep at the wheel it will begin to cause public outrage. The people will turn to their elected officials and ask, "Why aren't you protecting us? Isn't that why we elected you? What is being done about this?"

Yet if the government clamps down too tightly on the industry then they will begin to choke off the nation's economy and create even more congestion on the roadways which will cause even greater outrage amongst the voting citizens. So how does the government achieve this tricky balance? It's a combination of quelling the public outrage and keeping the law-breaking below an acceptable level.

Lets say that there is a major accident involving a tractor trailer. Any experienced driver will tell you that often times after such an accident occurs, especially if it is deemed the be the fault of the truck driver and the news reporters are covering the accident extensively, the state in which the accident occurred will have a BOAT LOAD of police agencies and DOT enforcement out on the prowl for the next few days or a week where they are clearly in the public eye. This let's people know that something is being done about it.

It's a simple matter of quelling the public outrage.

The general public has a rather short memory when it comes to such things though. The news will cover the story for a day, maybe even two or three days, and then it will slide into the background behind the latest incredible news events and quickly be forgotten.

However, every time the public becomes outraged with the elected officials it puts another chink in their armor and over time can build up to tarnish their reputations as the "protectors of the people" and hurt their chances at re-election. So they would rather not be spending their time and goodwill trying to quell public outrage, they would rather prevent it altogether.

So the method they use to try to prevent companies and individual drivers from causing public outrage, yet still keeping the economy as strong and efficient as possible, is to monitor how often a company and its drivers are breaking the law and keep it at an acceptable level.

The DOT and other law enforcement agencies will monitor both the individual drivers on the roadways and the trucking companies themselves. As individual drivers are ticketed nationwide the number of tickets being issued, what the tickets are being issued for, and WHO they are being issued to is being closely tracked.

They will track the number of tickets that are being given for things like traffic, logbook, and equipment safety violations. On top of this they will examine the number and type of accidents that a company's drivers have been involved in. The DOT will also do small amounts of random auditing of logbooks at the offices of individual trucking companies.

The DOT basically has predetermined numbers of acceptable law-breaking limits based on percentages. What those exact numbers are is far less important than how they handle a company whose drivers are above these acceptable limits.

If an audit is done at a company and the DOT finds that too high of a percentage of logbooks are being found to have violations then the DOT can take a variety of actions ranging from a verbal warning to heavy fines to completely shutting down the company permanently.

In case you're wondering, yes a number of companies have been put completely out of business over the years for very high levels of violations. The same applies to a company's safety record, equipment violation record, and the number of traffic tickets being issued to the company's drivers.

Now here's where the whole system begins to work against the individual drivers. Not only can an individual driver lose his or her license for getting too many points on it from traffic violations, but if the DOT begins to find too many problems within a company they will demand that some sort of action is taken.

Now the DOT does NOT want to shut down a company. But they don't mind fining the company (don't mind it at all actually) and they don't mind seeing the company fire some of its drivers for having too many log violations, traffic violations, or accidents.

They want to allow the company and its drivers to break the laws in order to benefit everyone but not to the extent that too many accidents take place and threaten the well being of the economy and causing public outrage to threaten the career of elected officials.

So let's begin to tie this all together.

As a driver you are being paid by the mile. The trucking companies are also being paid by the mile. The more miles a driver can run in a given amount of time the more money that driver will make, the more money his company will make, the more efficiently your customer's freight will be moved, the more money the American industries will make, the less congested the roads will be, the smaller the shortage of drivers will be, the more efficiently the economy will function as a whole, and the happier the American people will be, giving the elected officials a better chance of being re-elected the next time around....making everybody just so damn happy!

RIGHT?

RIGHT!

However, go too far with the number of miles being driven and the drivers begin to wear out and the number of accidents begins to rise causing lost money for the driver, his or her company, their customers, the American industries, the American people, and thus causing the elected officials to come under scrutiny putting their careers in jeopardy making everybody just so damn miserable, RIGHT?

RIGHT!

So what is the solution to all of this? Well, we should probably just put in a system that lets drivers run as many safe miles as possible making everybody as happy as they can be without going too far by allowing them to run too many miles causing too many accidents which makes everybody unhappy, RIGHT?

RIGHT!

Ok, so lets do that ok?

OK!

Well, do it then, ok?

OK. DONE!

WHAT????

DONE!

"WAAAAAAAAAAAAAIT A MINUTE!!!!!" You're saying to yourself right now, "Is that the system that's already in place???? If he just sold me this book and made me read all of that crap just to come full circle for no reason I'm gonna SLAY HIM!"

Alright, don' freak out on me now....I'm not wasting your time. In fact you'll be relieved to know that understanding all of this is going to be to the basis for many of the decisions you're going to be making as a driver for the rest of your career.

Now lets go back to where we were before and continue discussing how you will deal with the people and systems within your own company. I believe we left off with your dispatcher.

Back To Your Dispatcher

Ok so we left off wondering what the problem was that was keeping us from getting the miles we had hoped to be getting. We know other people have been getting say 2800 miles per week but you're getting only maybe 1800 and every so often you are running out of hours on your logbook and having no choice but to reschedule appointments because of it.

So knowing what you know now you decide, "ok I'll just cheat. I'll keep running even though I'm out of hours and I'll just fudge my logbook so nobody really knows. That way everybody's happy!" CONGRATULATIONS! You've come to the same conclusion that most of the drivers in the industry have come to. But like always, there's a catch. A few of them actually. And they are quite serious.

For starters, sometimes you can pretty easily fudge the book, sometimes it's not so easy. It depends on what factors your company is going to look for and how often they are going to look. Sometimes you can fudge it in a way that nobody will notice, sometimes you'll have to take the chance that nobody is going to audit your logs. Seems like a bit of a conundrum doesn't it?

Well, it's a lot more serious than you know. For one, if you were to get into a serious accident there is a very, very good chance that the DOT investigation will involve auditing your logs. If you had been falsifying your logs you could be facing federal charges along with a whole slew of other lawsuits and legal issues. I was fortunate to have driven almost 1.5 million miles without ever having had an accident. I can't begin to tell you how fortunate I was. But many drivers are not so fortunate.

Now any smart company will be way ahead of the drivers on this one. They want you to cheat, and when a driver does, the company will gladly turn their head the other way...that is, until THEY find themselves in some sort of trouble. Well, they would NEVER tell you to cheat. They can clearly see from the miles you are running that you must be cheating, but as long as nobody is looking they'll let it go. But the moment you get in an accident or the DOT comes in for a random log audit, well, guess what your company is going to do? Yap, that's right, they're going to throw you under the bus.

Now I've got your attention don't I? Now you're starting to see the seriousness of the dilemma a driver faces. So let's get this straight....everybody wins if the driver cheats his logbook, but if he gets caught the company is going to claim innocence and blame the driver? YAP! Now how can they do that? Well, because the company's policies about the driver following all federal rules and regulations regarding the logbook are in writing. When you got hired at the company, you signed em. You put your name to paper taking responsibility for following the laws and you as a driver are solely responsible for the safe and legal operation of the truck.

But they KNEW you were cheating, right? YAP! And they benefited from you cheating, right? YAP! But you can't PROVE they knew. Besides, YOU are responsible for the safe and legal operation of the truck, not them.

So say the DOT comes in one day, does an audit, and finds you have been falsifying your logs in a serious manner for quite a period of time. They could easily tell your company that they will be facing severe fines for this type of behavior so to appease the DOT, they fire you. Does that get your company off the hook? Most of the time, pretty much so, yap.

WOW, that is SERIOUS BS you say???? Yeah, no sh*t sherlock. Why do you think I'm writing this book? It is a very, very serious dilemma for the driver. If you follow the laws you will lose a ton of money and won't get treated nearly as well by your company as the guys who are cheating. Because those guys are willing to take the risk and move more freight, making more money for their company, they will be given the heavy workload. Yet if you DO decide to cheat, YOU as a driver are risking your job, your money if you were to get caught and fined, your license and your career if you get too many violations, and even jail time if you get in a serious accident. So what should you do?

You have to decide that for yourself. I can't tell you what you should do. It's the cold, harsh reality of life as a truck driver and nearly every driver in the United States is faced with this dilemma. I wish there was a simple answer, but there's not.

As far a dealing with your dispatcher goes, he or she needs drivers who can move as much freight as possible. Some dispatchers and most managers receive bonuses for improvements in revenues, efficiencies, or some combination of the two. So the harder you work as a driver, the more the office personnel will benefit directly. That's the game....that's the way it's played. You can choose to participate or you can opt out, but you just can't change the rules. It's been this way for decades.

Now if you're gonna scream and yell and go into a tirade then please let me know because...well hell, we ALL enjoy watching a good freak-out!

The best thing you can do is decide how you would like to handle this scenario and stick to your guns. If you are consistent then at least your dispatcher and the load planners know what type of loads they can give you. Don't decide to run your brains out sometimes and then out of the blue decide you're gonna run by the book. If they've grown accustomed to counting on you running hard and they give you a “hot” load for an important customer and you decide to shut down two hours short of your delivery, YOU may get a chance to watch a good freak-out!

Actually what will generally happen if you piss-off the dispatchers and load planners is you will sit....and sit....and sit.....and sit. A couple days is usually a good punishment period. You'll be begging them for a load but it just seems there isn't any freight. Bummer how that works.

Another issue that comes up with certain dispatchers is the matter of who's the boss, you or your dispatcher? They certainly believe they are the boss. In all reality, most companies go by a system called “forced dispatch”. In other words, they're gonna tell you tell you what load you're going to haul, and you are going to haul it.

But companies are desperate for good drivers so if you can prove to them over a period of time that your are safe, hard working, and reliable then they will do their best to compromise with you. If you'll haul a lousy load for them every so often then they will reward you with consistently good miles, a lot of good runs, and respect and tolerance for you as a driver and a as a human being. Your home time, family life, temper, driving style, special requests, and other idiosyncrasies will be accepted in return for the great job you do for them time and time again. At least most of the time. There are of course exceptions and I'll have plenty of stories ahead to show you more of the lessons I've learned...the hard way of course.

On To My Next Job

Well, I quit that job I had and decided I'd try something local...dump trucks. I figured after being on the road for a couple years it was time for a change. I wanted to have a more normal home life for a change. I wanted to be able to do some things I couldn't do while traveling all the time. I had never driven a dump truck before so I found a local company in Charlotte, NC and went for it.

So my new job turned out to be an interesting one. I was actually working for a landfill which accepted construction materials only. No food was allowed to be dumped there which we were all thankful for indeed. The landfill owned a few dump trucks and driving one of those was my first priority. If they didn't have anything for the dump trucks to do I did a wide variety of other jobs.

The landfill had bulldozers, front-end loaders, track hoes, and both a three-wheeled and a four-wheeled Terex crusher. The boss also did clearing, grading, and hauling jobs around the area. I never knew what I was going to be doing from day to day.

Some days I would crush garbage, some days drive dump truck, some days load dirt with the track hoe, and some days a combination of the three. I was also responsible for hauling the equipment around on a flatbed I pulled with the dump truck.

The variety of work was pretty fun and kept things interesting but the pay was pretty awful so I decided it was time to go back on the road. Again I wanted to try something new. I had only driven a dry van over the road and a dump truck locally. I called a driver referral service and told them I was looking for a smaller company that went coast to coast and wanted something a bit different. They told me about a small food-grade tanker company out of Des Moines, IA that was looking for a driver. Food grade tanker? Huh... I never drover a tanker before and never drove over the road for a small company so I figured what the hell??? I gave em a call, sent my resume, and they said they'd give me a shot and I accepted. Des Moines, IA here I come!!! It turned out to be a pretty good job and a I learned a few good lessons along the way.

So I go off to Iowa, get my truck, and because I never drove a tanker before I went on the road with another driver for a week so he could show me how to run the pump and all the ins and outs of getting loaded, unloaded, and maintaining the temperature of the liquid when necessary.

So I go out on the road with another driver for a week and he shows me the ropes. Actually, there was nothing to it. Sometimes I had to pump the fluid out of my tanker and into the customer's storage tank. Sometimes the customer did it. The most important thing to remember was to open the lid before you began to pump off the load or the suction would collapse the tank. Not good. That would be about a $50,000 mistake. Luckily I never made that mistake.

I mentioned some of the discoveries I made during my year with this company regarding the advantages and disadvantages of pulling a tanker versus other types of trailers. I also discovered a lot about the differences between working at a small company versus a large one.

This company only had eleven drivers. We had one owner, who didn't know much about anything it seemed. We had one dispatcher, who was masterful and experienced in the food-grade tanker arena. Lastly, we had one secretary who the drivers never really dealt with.

Being a small company, we didn't have the money behind us, we didn't have the accounts set up with truck stops and customers, we didn't have spare tanks for drop and hooks, and we didn't have 24 hours dispatchers when we needed them. Yeah, you could call the owner or dispatcher at 3:00 a.m. but it better be a pretty damn good reason.

Just before I went to work at this company they had a secretary that stole a bunch of money from the company and nobody knew it for a while. She was writing checks from the company to her personal bank account instead of paying the bills. So the late fees starting piling up, the company's credit was ruined, and the company financially was barely hanging on by a thread. I had no idea at first but found out soon enough.

One day I went to a tank wash and they said they couldn't wash me out until they got some money from the company. Seems we were a bit behind. So I called the owner and told him what was going on and he took care of it. That was a bit odd to me because I had only worked for large companies until that point and they have so much money behind them that you just don't run into that. But no biggie I guess and on I went.

Well, turned out every time I had to get work done or a wash done I had to go through this aggravating process of paying them on the spot and at times waiting for dispatch to track down the owner or whatever. Also the owner never wanted to pay out a nickel for anything if he could help it so anytime I needed something done it was like pulling teeth! When you're out on the road driving your ass off day and night coast the coast the last thing you feel like dealing with is arguing with your own company over the necessity of getting something done. Trust me on this one.

Well, as time went on and the financial situation got worse the owner pushed harder and harder. He wanted us to run as hard as he could possibly push us. I can't blame him. He was hurting for money and struggling to keep the company alive. But there is only so much a driver can do before he's had enough, and finally the day had come that I had had enough.

I had run for six straight weeks and finally got the chance to go home. I expected to stay home at least five or six days and surely deserved to do so. I ran very, very hard and did an awesome job. Well, after two days at home the owner calls and tells me he scheduled a pickup for me the next day. I told him there was no way I was leaving after just two days at home and he said either I go pickup that load or he's gonna fly someone out to get my truck and pick up the load and I would be fired. The next day my truck had been picked up and I was on to my next adventure.

In later years I discovered that after a year of awesome service that owner had tried to blackball me. He put into the computer system that trucking companies use to look up your past records that I had abandoned his truck, which is a really, really bad thing to do. You never want to quit a job and leave the truck somewhere for a company to have to retrieve. That's a big strike against a driver. Well, his company went bankrupt soon after I was fired so I didn't know of any way to get in touch with that owner to get my record cleared. Thanks a lot buddy.

I learned a few good lessons at this company. First of all I really liked pulling a food-grade tanker. I never have worked for another tanker company after that but that's because I had plenty of other good opportunities. But given the right circumstances I'd certainly do it again.

Secondly I learned I don't like working for small companies. Now there's a lot of drivers that love small companies, but I prefer the variety of freight, different divisions, convenient accounts, and a whole host of other advantages that the big companies have.

Lastly, it was the first time (but certainly not the last time) I had been stabbed in the back by my own company. Now I'm a straight forward type of guy. If I do something that deserves punishment, banishment, or imprisonment (all of which I have deserved at several points in my life) I'll readily admit it. But the work I did for this company was outstanding and I certainly didn't deserve to be fired or blackballed.

The trucking industry is full of triumphs and tragedies and although I can't predict any specifics regarding the future I can tell you you will experience both at some point in your career, so expect it.

Back To Dealing With Your Own Company

Ok so as you can see, dealing with your dispatcher and deciding how you will handle your logbook and any other issues within your own company is a far more complicated endeavor than you might have guessed. We've covered a lot of ground already but there's more. Let's dive further into the affairs within your own company.

Tractor Assignments

Let's talk a little bit about how the larger companies handle tractor assignments. Small companies have far fewer tractors and often times you may not have much of a choice. In fact, you may get hired because they have one tractor not being used so they need one driver to fill it. But at the large companies they have a large fleet of tractors and often times they have two or even three different brands in their fleet.

Most of the time each terminal at a company will have one person in charge of “seating” drivers as they refer to it. His job is to keep a list of available equipment and a list of drivers needing equipment. So how do they decide who will get what? Believe it or not, most of the time its just random. You would think they would base it on your experience both in the industry and within your own company, the division you will be in, and the trucks you've been driving so far....as in you've paid your dues and now you've worked your way up to a nicer truck.

Yeah, that would be nice, but believe it or not it's usually just random. Many times I've seen brand new drivers come out of school and get a brand new tractor on day one with their first company and I've seen just as many drivers quit a company after a number of years because for whatever reason they still won't give them the type of truck they wanted. Now of course it's not like that at all companies, but most of the ones I've ever dealt with it is. Why?

The person in charge of assigning tractors gets bombarded with requests every day from dispatchers, managers, drivers, mechanics, recruiters, and even driver's spouses. Yet they don't have any control of what tractors will be available at any given time.

A company will be losing a lot of money if they have a lot of trucks sitting idly. You would think that a company with thousands of drivers would at least have a couple dozen tractors available at any given time but usually this isn't the case. With orientation classes making drivers available every day there is a constant flow of drivers entering and leaving the company every day.

Often times the list of available trucks is shorter than the list of drivers needing trucks. This helps keep a company efficient and hopefully profitable. It's not that drivers are waiting a week for a truck or anything like that. It's usually a day, maybe two at the most. So it usually works out to be first come first serve. You wait in line on the list and as trucks become available you'll get one.

Most of the time a company will not have any trucks more than a few years and they try to keep them in nearly brand new conditions so to them it shouldn't matter too much which truck they give you, they're all pretty similar.

In my experience they're right. As long as the maintenance program is a good one they will fix anything and everything that you find needs attention. So by the time you leave the terminal in your newly assigned truck it should be comfortable and in perfect working condition no matter the age and mileage on it.

Now I can't tell you how many hundreds of drivers I've seen over the years absolutely OBSESS over which type of truck they're going to get. I've driven 'em all and although there are certain ones that I like better than others it just isn't enough of a difference to worry too much about it.

A lot of drivers will show up for their first day of orientation and the very first thing out of their mouth is, "I won't even drive for this company if I don't get a ...(truck of their choice). My recruiter promised me one and I won't drive anything else."

Remember earlier when I mentioned jumping off the Empire State Building and landing squarely on your face? Well, this is another example of someone who should do that. Please don't stress yourself out over which truck you get. Just take what they give you and go through it thoroughly to make sure everything appears to be working properly...wipers, mirror heaters, 12 volt plugs in the cab and sleeper, the heat, air conditioning, and the fans both in the cab and sleeper, power windows and locks, all the lights, turn signals, and anything else you can think of.

Ask the shop if any maintenance has just been done to it and when the next work is scheduled to be done. If everything is in working order, the truck has been inspected, and no other work is scheduled to be done then the truck should be just fine. Now of course there are some parts on the truck that you can never tell when they are about to break like the alternator, starter, fuel pump, or something in the transmission.

These things can go at any time and there's nothing anybody can do about that. But please don't freak yourself out over which truck you get. I'm telling ya it just doesn't make that big of a difference. You want something to obsess over? Obsess over which dispatcher you're going to get. Now THAT is something that really, really matters.

Getting Repairs Done

Since we're on the subject of tractors, let's talk about getting them fixed. A large company will have its own shops and mechanics at the terminals...at least at some of the terminals. A small company may have their own shop or they may have a local shop nearby that does all of their work for them. Unfortunately a lot of diesel mechanics don't get paid very well and it's not uncommon to wait a day or two to even get the tractor into a shop, whether it be one of your company's shops, a general repair shop on the road, or an actual truck dealership.

The mechanics aren't usually in much of a hurry (I'm actually being pretty nice here) and the shops get pretty backed up with work. Getting repairs done is one of the most frustrating aspects of life on the road. You are usually get paid by the mile or by the load so sitting there waiting for your truck to get fixed isn't making you any money.

Now most companies will give you a little bit of money for food and layover time and will pay for your motel if you need one, but usually they'll give you just enough money to eat and drink your sorrows away. In the end you're often left with nearly nothing.

My general rule of thumb for getting major repairs done on the road was to tell your company you're going to need a hotel....trust me, you usually will. Now small repairs like an alternator or starter, tire changes, lights, and things of that nature will usually get done within a few hours while you wait. But if the truck quits running and needs to be towed or the repair is going to be something major just expect to spend the night in a motel.

Relax, get a nice shower, watch some TV, walk to a nearby bar if you like, order a pizza, get an awesome night's sleep, and be prepared to get back to running hard the next day. Your life won't be ruined if you lose a day or two for repairs. You can easily make up those lost miles in the coming days and weeks. But a nice relaxing 24 hours in a hotel can be incredibly refreshing.

Take advantage of it. The company is paying for it anyways. Enjoy yourself. It's a great excuse to do nothing.

Now many large companies will have accounts set up with truck stops to get work done. I've found that it's usually much, much faster to get small repairs done on the road than it is at your company's terminals. Especially oil changes, known as PM's (preventive maintenance), and small repairs like tires, alternators, lights, etc.

Often times you can pull in without any wait whatsoever and an hour later you're rolling again. While you wait, go into the truck stop, take a shower, get a good meal, catch up on your paperwork, and get yourself ready to roll when the truck is finished. Often times the truck stops will offer you a free shower or meal while you're getting the work done so ask them.

Now, not only is the work getting done faster at the truck stops but you even get free stuff while they're doing it. Bonus! Efficient use of your time on the road is key. The more driving you do the more money you make so make good use of your down time so you can focus on driving when the truck and the freight are available.

Talk with your maintenance department and find out all of their procedures. They will tell you they prefer to do the work in their own shops instead of on the road but it isn't the mechanics, maintenance supervisors, and office managers that are losing time, money, and being inconvenienced while you're waiting for them to do the work, its you.

As a driver you must be aware of how your actions affect your company, but keep in mind that YOU have the hardest job of anybody so you have to look out for yourself. If you enjoy the idea of getting a hotel once in a while or you can make better use of your time by getting the work done at a truck stop then do it. It won't happen too often anyways and it can make a big difference to you.

Besides, if you're happy, well-fed, and well-rested you're going to be a harder-working, safer driver so helping yourself can also be helping your company at the same time. They often aren't going to look at it that way, but they've never lived on the road, so they really wouldn't know would they? Exactly.

Competition

The North American trucking industry, more precisely the industry in the United States and Canada (but possibly to include Mexico soon in a big way), is one of the most competitive industries on earth. I always use the expression hyper-competitive. I'm not even certain that hyper-competitive is a real expression, but it sounds cool.....kinda zoomy!!! But as a new driver, the competition between companies should not really concern you too much just yet. You should definitely NOT be considering buying your own truck without a few years in the industry first.

The only exception I can think of is maybe a situation where your family, maybe your parents or aunts and uncles, have owned their own trucks over the years and you will be under their guidance with your own truck. But for the vast majority of new drivers you should not be considering buying your own truck and learning to compete in this industry while at the same time learning to drive the truck and handle your new life on the road. It's just too much all at once. But what you will be concerned with from day one is the competition for equipment, freight, and possibly opportunities to join different divisions within your own company.

As an employee of any company you should be aware of the fact that what's good for the company is often times good for you, and visa-versa. Not always of course, but if you want to keep your job you should be doing what you can to promote the well being of both yourself and your company. Simple enough.

However, as a driver at any company, especially the larger ones, you will actually be competing with the other drivers in your own company. You should approach this competition with integrity, not dirty tactics, but make no bones about it...the other drivers in your company are your peers AND your competitors.

For all intents and purposes you can look at your company as having a given amount of drivers using a given amount of equipment to haul a given amount of freight at any particular time. For example, today your company may have 5000 drivers, 5000 tractors, 7000 trailers, and 3000 loads. Keep in mind that you will have a certain number of loads that take more than one day to deliver, so not all drivers will need a new load everyday.

Let's get more specific. Let's say that today your company has 2100 drivers that will need a new load but only 1950 new loads available. There are a lot of things you can do to make sure you're NOT one of those 150 drivers that aren't going to make any money today. It starts from day one at your first company and will be a never ending process throughout your entire career. Let's take a look at how this works and some of the things you can do.

For starters put yourself in your company's shoes. Your company has made gigantic investments in equipment and employees with the assumption that they will be able to get enough freight to be profitable overall. It's a gigantic commitment. When they hired you the deal was pretty simple....they'll supply you with a truck and trailer and then they will find freight for you to haul. All you have to do is haul the loads they give you, safely and on time, and they'll pay you well for it. Sounds good so you join the company and off you go.

Of course they made that same deal with all the drivers at the company. So now all of you get your trucks and head out there to get it done.

In order to get freight your company has to hire salesman. These salesman build contacts and go out there in a very competitive environment to try to get enough freight to keep everybody moving, and do it at a price that the company can be profitable. Well, the more promises your salesman can make to the customers, like keeping spare trailers at their facility, hauling loads on short notice, and guaranteeing that a certain percentage of the loads will be picked up and delivered on time, the more money your company can charge the customers to haul their freight.

Often times it's especially beneficial to both your company and to your customers if the two sides can agree to terms on a contract. That way your company will be assured to have a certain amount of loads available at a certain price and your customer knows they can get their freight hauled under certain concrete terms. It takes some of the unpredictability out of doing business for both companies.

Being in business has a lot of ups and downs. It can be highly volatile at times. Anytime you can remove some of that volatility you improve the likelihood that your company will be successful into the future.

Here's an example:

Say your company, Alpha, knows their cost of hauling freight is about $1.05 per mile. They contact a manufacturing company, Bravo, that needs anywhere from 5 to 15 loads hauled per day, overnight, on short notice to a group of customers it serves. Your company already has plenty of drivers available to haul even the maximum number of loads they may need each day and they also have enough spare trailers that they can keep at Bravo's premises to allow Bravo to load them on their own schedule.

Bravo knows their cost of doing business and figures they can pay up to $1.60 per mile to have their freight hauled to their customers. So both sides sit down and agree to a price of $1.45 per mile for each load. Perfect!

Now Bravo doesn't have to worry about being able to get their freight to their customers on time for a reasonable price, and your company, Alpha, knows that they will be getting several loads per day from Bravo at a price that will be profitable for them.

This type of contract is common in the industry. Larger trucking companies have a multitude of contracts set up along with the ability to find more freight from other sources anytime they need it. Here's where you come in.

Obviously your company has to fulfill the terms of their contracts and also the terms of any individual loads that they acquire from day to day. The salesman make promises that you as a driver must fulfill. If you don't, it's pretty obvious what will happen. Your company can be penalized or can loose these contracts altogether. Happens all over the country everyday. Companies gain or lose contracts based on price, performance, other services they can or can not provide, or a combination of these variables.

Now, your company has a large pool of loads to haul and a large pool of drivers to choose from everyday. Believe me, your company keeps track of their driver's reliability records and knows how important and difficult each of their loads are to haul. No company is going to give highly important, difficult loads to drivers that are unreliable. Once in a great while they may have no choice for one reason or another, but overall they aren't careless about which drivers get which loads.

So say for instance there are three drivers sitting empty in a certain area and only two highly valuable loads are available. Yap, you guessed it, the two most reliable drivers are going to be making money that day, the third will be watching John Wayne movies at the nearest truck stop all day.

But it goes a step further than that. Maybe there's three empty drivers and only two loads available, yet neither of the loads is too difficult or critical. Your company is still going to give the loads to the best two drivers available. Just as you would expect they are going to treat their better drivers better.

Now take into consideration the discussion we had earlier about cheating the logbook. What if all three drivers are good, reliable drivers but the two loads absolutely MUST be delivered overnight. Say two of the three drivers are known to be willing to cheat the book in order to get the job done, the third has been known to shut down when he runs out of hours. Again, the company isn't going to risk it.

You never know what circumstances may arise that would cause the drivers to run out of hours that day....traffic, weather, breakdowns, delays at the shipper, etc. So the two loads are going to go to the drivers which have the best possibility of making the pickup and delivery on time. Your company can't afford to risk it.

Yet none of this will likely be discussed. Your company isn't going to say, “Hey, I don't care about your logbook, just get that load delivered on time.” Nope. What they're going to say is, “Hey this is an important customer and this load HAS to be delivered on time. Can you do it?” If you want to make the money, you're going to do it. If you're already a super rich John Wayne fan you might say, “Nope, I don't have the hours.” In that case, enjoy your movies! The other two guys will get the loads if they're willing to get the job done.

Another nice tip is with regard to finding empty trailers. Depending on the company you work for you may or may not have a hell of a time finding an empty trailer to use for your next load after dropping your loaded trailer at the customer. Most companies won't even assign you a load until you find an empty trailer first. Your company will help you locate one...eventually....but here's a scenario to consider.

You drop your loaded trailer at the delivery and find there's another driver from your company already sitting at the same delivery location. He's sitting there without a trailer which right away has you thinking, “oh great....there's no empty trailers here.” Sure enough you're right. He already let his dispatcher know he needs them to find him an empty and they said they'll get back to him. Now you call in and let them know you've dropped your loaded trailer and need an empty also. If they're having trouble finding him one it may take a while before they get back to you.

Even worse is the possibility that you two are the only drivers in the area and there's only one load available that day. Guess what? Whoever comes up with an empty trailer first will be assigned the load. You don't want to sit there waiting for hours if you can help it so how do you prevent this from happening? Simple:

In your day to day driving, keep a list of the names, addresses, and if you can get it the phone numbers of any locations you notice your company has dropped trailers. Just simply keep your list organized by state. Believe me, this has saved the day dozens of times!

I can't count the number of times I've arrived at my delivery to find as many as five or more drivers lined up along the fence waiting for hours on end for an empty trailer location to be sent to them. After talking to them for a few minutes I tell them I'm going up the road to get something to eat and immediately bolt to the nearest location that I know we may have trailers.

When I arrive and find an empty trailer I grab one, let my dispatcher know I'm ready for my next load assignment, and wait for the assignment to come through. Then I let my dispatcher know there are several trucks up the road looking for empty trailers and I tell him how many I've found at the location I'm at. Then I'm off and running.

You'll be so glad you kept that list the first time this works for you....and it will. Like I said, it's a competitive environment. If you want to get ahead you have to work hard, be safe and reliable, and in the case of this last example, be more thorough than the other drivers.

One last thing you can try to do once you've proven yourself to be safe and reliable is to try to get dispatch to plan your next load before you deliver the one you have. I promise you, though, it may be very difficult to get them to do this until you have thoroughly proven yourself because once a load has been assigned to you it may cause a lot of headaches in the office if you can't fulfill that commitment.

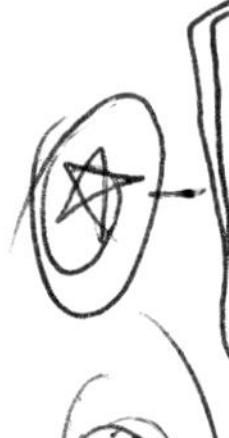

If you've done all of these things and you've had a couple of slow weeks in a row, ask your dispatcher if he would mind you calling his boss or maybe even the next boss above his in order to beg and plead for some better freight. Remember, your dispatcher probably doesn't have too much say in who gets assigned what loads, but his boss might. Just make it clear to your dispatcher that you're not calling the bosses to complain about him or her, you just want to see if somebody can pull some strings to get you rolling.

If you get along well with your dispatcher and he or she has done everything in their power to get you freight but nothing is working they won't mind you taking the initiative to get some freight. You're not doing your dispatcher any harm. You're just doing whatever you can think of to do to help yourself.

When you do get in touch with the boss, make it clear that you're not calling to complain about your dispatcher. It seems to you that dispatch is doing all they can to help you but nobody is listening to them so you're just looking for a little bit more help. I've done this a million times and it usually works really well. Again, you just have to know who to call when you need something. If somebody doesn't have the authority to make something happen you have to find out who does and talk to them.

Getting a little help from the bosses will also help them get to know you better. Take a few minutes to talk to them about how things are going for you and put in a good word for your dispatcher if you feel he or she is doing a good job. Normally the bosses hear more complaints than anything else so putting in a good word and showing your appreciation for the help they're giving you can really go a long ways. You don't have to be a kissy-ass, just be positive.

If you really want someone to help you out with something, the most powerful force that will work in your favor won't be fear, threats, or demanding some sort of special treatment you probably haven't earned anyhow. The best chance you'll have of getting good results from somebody is if they WANT to help you. If they like you and they're pleased with the job you're doing they will want to do what they can for you.

Screaming and yelling, threatening, and other types of crazy behavior will usually work against you, not for you. Think about it....would you rather help one of your friends with something or some arrogant jerk you can't stand the sight of? Exactly. Keep that in mind.

When freight gets slow and it comes down to the harsh reality that some drivers are going to be making money today and some are going to be sitting around with nothing to do, you have to stay ahead of the game if you want to keep rolling. Keep pushing your dispatcher to keep you moving. Don't be too overbearing, but make it clear that you really want the miles. You'll be amazed at how many lazy drivers there are. Some don't really care to run that hard, some do. Keep on top of things and most of all just do an awesome job and you'll find that most of the time you'll be well taken care of.

We've done a good job of covering a lot of the issues you will be facing in the day to day operations within your own company. Now let's take a look at some of the issues you will be facing when handling the customers you will be serving.

Hauling Freight And Handling Customers

Wow, look at how far we've come. You're a real truck driver now. Graduated from school, got hired, finished your training, and now you're learning the ropes and making money. Now that you've just learned a whole lot of tips, tricks, ideas, expectations, and realities regarding you own company to help you get along better and get more freight sent your way, we'll turn our focus to helping you understand how to deal with the customers you'll be hauling the freight for.

It doesn't matter how much freight you are able to get from your company, if you can't figure out how to get to the customers on time and get loaded and unloaded early sometimes you just aren't going to end up with as many miles as you would have otherwise. Let's get to it.

Let's cover the process in the order it will happen. You're sitting at a truck stop empty and waiting for your next assignment. You hear the satcomm beep (satcomm is satellite communications – basically a satellite based email in your truck that allows you to type messages back and forth to your company) and your load information begins to come through. Awesome....you'll be making some money today!

You have the customer and load information and it's time to get moving. First of all you have to figure out how to get there and what route to take! Included in your load information will usually be directions to get to the shipper. OH, that's GREAT, RIGHT? No. Why NOT? Because if you follow the directions you are given, exactly the way they are written, I would estimate that about 80% of the time you will NOT get to your destination.

The directions have been put in there by other drivers that have gone to this customer and for whatever reason they are usually wrong. How in the world could a driver wind up putting the wrong directions in the computer when there will be tons of other drivers relying on them in the future? Hell if I know. It's one of those puzzling things you can't completely make sense out of.

Sometimes it's a typo, sometimes it's simply confusing left and right, sometimes landmarks change (for instance 'take a right at the second light' used to be correct but now a new traffic light has been installed and the turn is actually at the third light), and some drivers are just idiots that couldn't find their way out of a paper bag. I've actually had a couple drivers tell me they've purposely put in the wrong directions because they hate their company and the drivers are a bunch of jerks anyway. Thanks a lot.

So what should you do? Couple of options. First, the most obvious....call the customer. Take a look at the map and find the town they're located in so you can tell them which direction you are coming from. When you get someone on the phone be aware of a couple things. First of all, some people are afraid to admit they don't know something because it will make them look stupid.

These people will TRY to give you directions even though they really aren't sure. Listen, don't be afraid of hurting their feelings. If you sense this is happening, be nice but be firm. Explain to them that one wrong turn in a truck that's 65 feet long and 13 ½ feet high can be disastrous.

Low bridges and restricted routes can lead to accidents and tickets and you would appreciate it if they would try to find somebody that is absolutely certain of the directions. At that point they will often times be relieved that the pressure is off of them and will gladly find somebody else to help you.

Now once you get someone on the phone that's certain, be aware that most of the time these people have other things on their mind and might accidentally say something wrong, like “left” instead of “right”. As they are giving you the directions, repeat them out loud as you are writing them. You can't begin to imagine how many times people will say, “OH, did I say left? I'm sorry, I meant right”. I'm telling you, this happens all the time. They're distracted, that's all.

Also try to get as many landmarks along the way as you can, especially at the turns. They might say something like, “take a left at the third light. There's a statue on the corner.” Not only is it easy to see the landmark coming pretty far up the road, but maybe it's actually at the fourth light and they were mistaken. No problem. People are much better with landmarks than they are at counting lights and estimating distances. They don't count lights on the way to work everyday, they look for landmarks. So chances are if you have landmarks at the corners you'll be alright.

Again, happens all the time.

Now once the person is finished with the directions, repeat the entire thing back to them. Say something like, “ok, so let me make sure I wrote this down correctly....” and repeat the entire thing. You will often catch even more mistakes this way and get some extra tips and landmarks along the way. Do NOT be concerned with the three minutes of their time you are taking up by being thorough.

If they make one simple mistake it can easily cost you fifteen to thirty minutes (yeah, and I've had worse than that) or even lead to a ticket, an accident, or you may not arrive until after they close for the day and you miss that day's load altogether. Take your time and be thorough. Believe me it's time well spent.

Lastly, confirm that it's ok for trucks to take the route they have given you. Remember, they don't drive a big rig to work, they drive a car. Low bridges and restricted routes are of no concern to them. Often times somebody can give you good directions for a car to take but they never really thought about whether or not a truck can safely take that route. Make sure you point this out to them.

Another great tool, and one that will soon be used by most every driver nationwide, is GPS. I highly suggest you get one. If you don't have a laptop or a GPS unit I highly recommend you buy an inexpensive laptop and get the GPS software for it. The large screen is far better than the smaller screens on stand-alone units and you will then have a full-blown computer with you for surfing the Internet, sending and receiving email, and a whole host of other activities you'll really enjoy.

We're going to get into the multimedia entertainment opportunities a little later on. But for now, a laptop and GPS are the best tool a trucker could ever have.

My rule of thumb for directions to a customer is, “two out of three”. Of the three different ways to get directions to a customer: phone, your company's directions, and GPS, I always made sure that at least two of them matched up perfectly. If two different sets of directions were the same you were almost guaranteed to have the proper ones. Not always of course, but short of the customer driving their building to you, this is about as good as it's gonna get.

Ok, so you have the directions and you're almost ready to roll. Let's assume you still have the shipper on the phone and you've just finished getting the directions. While you have them on the phone be sure to confirm the appointment time and find out a couple of other things. First of all, if you have an opportunity to arrive early for your appointment, ask them if it's ok to come in early. Some places don't want you too early because they don't have much room for trucks to park.

Also find out if they have trailers from your company already on site that they will be loading or will they be loading the trailer you're bringing with you? If they already have a trailer that they will be loading it will give you a lot more flexibility with your arrival time.

Next ask them if there is any chance you can be loaded early. Most of the time there is at least a chance. That's all you can hope for...a chance. At this point even if they say you won't be loaded early but it's ok to arrive early if you would like...DO IT! A lot of times you can talk them into loading you early anyways. It sure can't hurt your chances of getting out of there on time anyways.

Finally ask them if there is anything special you will be required to have for this load. Is this load a hazmat load? Do you need load bars or straps? Does the trailer have to be a certain size? Are there any load numbers your company was supposed to give you? This one is quite common. Companies will often attach a number to each load.

That number will be used for their internal paperwork, your company's paperwork, and their customer's paperwork. It also acts like a security pass so that they know you really are the driver that is supposed to be picking up that load. NOW you are finally ready to roll.

It's a really good idea to make sure you have something to eat and drink with you. Sitting and waiting for hours and hours at a customer is unfortunately all too common. Something to read would really be nice too.

Use your best judgment to find the safest, surest route to get there. Do NOT worry about finding little shortcuts that will save you ten or fifteen minutes. Stick to the truck routes and the directions you were given. Often times you will see these possible shortcuts. It's tempting, at least until you've learned the hard way five hundred times and come upon low bridges, restricted routes, or simply made a wrong guess.

You will waste tons of time, be totally aggravated, and could possibly get a ticket or get into an accident. Forget it, I'm telling ya. Take the sure route. Remember, this is your career now.

You will hopefully be doing this for many, many years to come. If you are the type to take chances, sooner or later the numbers are going to catch up to you and you're going to pay the price. At this point I've driven around 1.5 million safe miles over a period of 13 ½ years. My excellent record isn't luck. It's because I made smart decisions. Always taking the safest, surest route has been a very big part of my success.

Ok so you've arrived at the customer safe and sound. Let's discuss some of the things you can do at this point to try to speed things up so you can get rolling.

The faster you can get loaded and get rolling the better off life will be for you. Often times once you get loaded you have a given amount of time to make it to your delivery. The quicker you're loaded the more time you will have to spare. If you're the type of driver that's looking to make all the money you can make a lot of times they will give you a load that you could run in one day but they're giving you two days to do it. Maybe you're scheduled to load at 11:00 a.m. on Monday and the load goes 750 miles for an 8:00 a.m. Wednesday morning delivery.

If you can get loaded pretty quickly on Monday you can run hard and deliver Tuesday morning. Can you do it legally by the logbook? I very much doubt it. But I'm not telling you what to do. I'm giving you the information so you can decide how to run your own career. Let's assume you want to make all of the money you can just for fun.

You pull into the shipper at 9:00 a.m. and you're going to try to get them to load you early. Remember what I said earlier: the best chance you have for someone to do you a favor is if they WANT to do you a favor. So with this in mind you approach the shipping department.

What I always do is explain my situation honestly(or with a bit of exaggeration as insurance). I tell them, "I know my appointment isn't until 11:00 but I came in early hoping I could get loaded a bit early. If I can get this load delivered tomorrow instead of Wednesday, my dispatcher has me set up on a load that ships around noon on Tuesday.

If you can somehow find a way to get me going a bit sooner that would be a really big deal to me. If you can't I understand, but if you can I'd really, really appreciate it. It'd be a really big deal. If you don't need me for anything I'll just be waiting in the truck while you're loading me. Thanks a lot."

Simple enough, right? You wouldn't believe how many drivers, even experienced drivers, go storming into a place demanding immediate service, threatening to leave the place and not take the load, and insulting the dockworkers for being slow, lazy, and uncaring if they won't load them early. What, are you kidding me? Do you really think you can get any kind of results that way? You're gonna sit out there in that parking lot and ROT if they can get away with it, and some places CAN. But why on Earth would they want to help you out?

You're a JERK! And you're not their boss.

Very, very few people understand or appreciate truck drivers and how difficult our jobs are. Honestly, a lot of people care more about the color of Mr Roger's sweater. Your best chance of getting them to help you out is to help them understand your situation and treat them with respect. Be the type of person they enjoy being around and maybe, just maybe they'll want to help you out. That's the best you can hope for. It won't always work, but more times than not it will.

For quite a number of years I ran regional routes. I'd be out five days and home two on average. If you get a scenario like the one I just went through and you can get loaded and make the delivery early, it can be a huge, huge difference in your pay that week. You may get 2800 miles that week if you can get a couple of places to load or unload you early. You may only get 1700 if you can't.

At, say, thirty eight cents per mile you're talking a difference of $418 THAT WEEK! That's as much as the total paycheck for a lot of people each week! Now multiply that by about 50 working weeks per year and you can see what a gigantic amount of extra money we're talking about here. It's huge!

So if you feel you can get loaded in time to deliver early, immediately call the consignee (that's the ridiculous word they use for the place you're delivering) and give them the same exact story. I'd say 80%-90% of the time the customers will be glad to get their shipment early.

Some won't be able to take it early because they don't have the storage space or they already have too many trucks scheduled on the day you wanted to deliver, but usually they'll take their freight as soon as you can get it to ‘em.

The Driver's Responsibility

Let's talk about what exactly the driver is responsible for when it comes to hauling freight. To be on the safe side let's assume that the driver is responsible for absolutely everything unless I specifically say otherwise.

And I probably won't say otherwise.

A typical story you'll hear a driver tell after his truck has tipped over is, "I was going around the curve on the offramp and the load shifted causing the truck to tip." And I believe every word of this story almost every time because that's exactly what usually happened, except they left out a couple of details....what they should have said was, "I was going too fast around the curve on the offramp and the load, that I said was loaded properly and was safe for travel, shifted causing the truck to tip."

Couple of really important things to note here. The first one simply relates to how fast a truck can go around a curve. Well, there's two ways to find out. One, you could hire an engineer and give them the numerical details involving weight, center of gravity height, turn radius, etc and a few simple calculations later you have the exact speed a specific truck can go around a particular curve.

The easier way is too just get in a truck and find out the "real world" way. DON'T do this. NOT EVEN ONCE!

Often times when a truck tips over on an interstate highway ramp the driver knew when he took the exit that he was going way too fast but figured he'd find a way to get it slowed down really quickly. Misjudgments in a big rig can be really, really bad sometimes.

Really bad.

Taking chances and making assumptions can be equally terrible. I realize that it's out of order to cover this topic right now but I don't care....nothing in the world is more important to any trucker than safety. There is no bad time to mention it.

The other important point here is the focus of this section....the driver is totally one hundred percent responsible for the safe and proper loading of his truck. Once the shipper puts the freight on your trailer and you decide it's road worthy then it now becomes your responsibility. Does this mean that if someone loads your truck in such a way that you're not happy with then you don't have to haul it until they do it your way???

YES! That's exactly what that means!

If you say you don't feel it will scale properly or you don't feel it's loaded in a way that will be safe to move, you simply don't move the truck an inch! They may try to convince you, "oh, we load all the trucks this way and nobody says anything." Then you tell em, "good for you and them, but I don't care what anybody else does with their trucks. I need my truck loaded my way because I'm responsible for it, not you."

The shipper usually won't argue with you though. They know you're responsible so if you say you want it a certain way they do it. You don't have to make this into a big argument. It's your responsibility so the truck doesn't move until you say it's ready to move. Period. If they have any concerns let them call your company and complain. Your company will just tell them the same thing you already told them anyhow. So don't stress it. It will be done your way.

Again, just don't leave the shipper until you're happy. I've had numerous shippers try to talk me into letting them load it a certain way. I didn't stress, I didn't argue. I just explained that in my experience I've found certain methods that work well and so I'd prefer they load it the way I'm comfortable with. Try to avoid making enemies on the dock. Rarely will you benefit from that scenario.

The dockworkers will just want to make life miserable for you if they can, and believe me they usually can. Real miserable. So be calm, talk it over, and if they do happen to continue with giving you a hard time gladly give them your company's phone number and let them call your company and talk to your boss. No biggie.

Hazmat Routing

Let's talk briefly about what routes you are able to take with a HAZMAT load. You'll recall that I mentioned earlier about routing yourself to customers. If you wind up somewhere you don't belong in a truck you're going to get ticketed and YOU are going to pay it. Even if you follow the routing your company gives you, they aren't responsible. You are.

One time I went down a road I wasn't supposed to be on. It was a side street next to the customer and there wasn't a sign visible saying "no trucks" until after I had already made the turn. A cop just happened to be there and pulled me over.

I told him I was following the directions that their secretary had given me and she apparently didn't know it wasn't a truck route. I told him that SHE probably takes that route to work and just figured it would work for me. I said I was sorry and I would inform the company of that situation to avoid other drivers taking that route in the future.

I lied. He let me go.

I'm not saying you should lie. I'm saying you do have to be aware that these things will happen every so often.

So if you get a HAZMAT load be aware that you are responsible for finding the proper routing. In the beginning of your Trucker's Road Atlas you will find a section that lists all of the phone numbers for the DOT in each state. You can call each state on your route and tell them the route you are considering and they will tell you if it's ok for a HAZMAT load or not.

Get a name from the person you get the information from though. If you do get incorrect info from the DOT you can surely use that as a defense. But don't count on anything. Be sure of your route before you take it. Don't guess.

Unfortunately, there's another general rule you can expect as a truck driver...if anything goes wrong the driver will be the one who pays the price. Wow, GREAT advertisement for pursuing a career in the industry ya know? But it's true.

For instance, the load is overweight. You pay the fine. There's a traffic jam you're stuck in for 2 hours? Time lost for you. Sit in a shipper's parking lot for six hours waiting to be loaded? Shame for you. Winter storm rolls through and you have to shut down for a day or two? Hope you brought some books with you. You cheat the logbook and get caught? Hand over the money. Your pay will revolve around getting the job done.

You get paid by the mile....no miles, no money. You get the same amount no matter how long it takes.

The advantage of course is that you can make a lot more money if you want to because you can run more miles when they are available. But every time you get delayed it's basically tough luck for you. Focus on keeping things moving. The money will keep flowing as long as the truck keeps rolling. But remember, if you take chances you are bound to lose out sometimes. Accidents, tickets, suspensions, and anything else that will keep you from rolling will also cost you money.

So don't run so hard that you get in trouble all the time but don't sit around so much that you don't make good money. Find the balance that works for you. Listen to how other drivers approach their jobs, but do what you feel is right for you. I don't care if someone has been driving for thirty years. There will be things they do that you would simply hate. And visa-versa.

Advice leads to great ideas, but don't feel you have to do things the way somebody else is doing them. There is always a number of ways to be successful as a driver. Find the ways that work best for you.

Entertainment And Technology

Let's lighten things up a bit and talk about the technological tools and entertainment that's available for you on the road. Most people would never guess that modern trucks are like a rolling technology convention. You have a multitude of toys and tools that are based on satellite, radio wave, RFID, radar, CB, camera, wireless Internet, and cell tower technologies.

I love technology and used about every form of tool and entertainment I could get my hands on! If you aren't able to do your job efficiently and safely and you can't enjoy yourself on the road, your career as a driver will be a short and miserable one. Let's give you an idea of what's out there these days for you.

Let's start with tools, and the most important of all tools a driver can have in my opinion....a GPS. Earlier I touched on it, now let's go into a bit more detail.

For starters, GPS is simply a satellite-based locating device that will pinpoint where you are on a map. It can be incredibly accurate...often times within 50 feet or so. The satellites were put up there by the military and the service was made available to the public free of charge. You can buy a stand-alone unit or you can buy the software and antenna to use with a laptop computer.

I strongly suggest getting the version for your laptop because the screen is so much bigger, which is incredibly important when you're trying to follow it turn for turn, and the laptop will be a great addition to your trucking life both as a tool and for entertainment.

With GPS you have the ability to punch in your starting and finishing location and it will give you the route to take based on a number of different calculations the software will do for you. Be careful though...these routes do not take into consideration the fact that you are driving a truck. It will not warn you of low bridges and restricted routes. You have to be aware of those yourself.

It's simple to change the routing to fit your situation. Once the route is set you just simply follow it on the map. The computer will tell you where to turn. It even has voice technology built in so it can speak to you as you are driving and will reroute you if you make a wrong turn.

Seriously, if you're one of those anti-technology people and you would rather suffer with the old ways instead of taking a few minutes to learn the new, again I point you to the old way of relieving your stress from the top of the Empire State Building. You'll die, but that's better than having to learn third-grade level computer skills isn't it? Oh brother.

GPS is one of the best tools you will ever find as a truck driver and they improve these systems every year. If you could only buy one tool to help you on the road, this should be the one. Once you've used GPS you will quickly consider it a necessity, not a luxury. I guarantee it.

Wireless Internet is another incredible tool. If you already own a laptop with GPS it's simple to use the laptop for all kinds of things like email, web surfing, and tracking loads and expenses. One of my favorite things to do was to use Google Earth and bring up satellite images of the place I was going to. What a huge help that was. Then you know exactly what the area looks like – where potential parking spots are and potential hazards. You can often find landmarks to help you find your destination.

Of course everybody is familiar with CB radios. Don't even think about driving without one. It will help you find out a lot of information - road and traffic conditions, appropriate routing, directions to places, DOT inspections, low bridges, weigh station status, weather, and when it's your turn to back into a dock at a customer amongst a multitude of other things.

You don't need a top of the line radio, but you want a good one. If you spend between $100-$200 on a well known brand like Cobra, Uniden, or Galaxy you'll be fine. That's all I ever used . Also get a decent antenna. Spend about $15-$30 dollars on one and read the directions for tuning in your SWR. It stands for Standing Wave Ratio and basically matches up your radio with your antenna to get the best results. If you don't want to mess with it too much just go to any CB repair shop near one of the truck stops and let them help you out.

They may try to talk you into all kinds of stuff like getting bigger finals, getting it 'peaked and tuned', and noise effects. This stuff will all be fine to do one day down the road but for now just worry about getting a decent radio, antenna, and tuning in the SWR. If you get that taken care of you'll be in great shape. The fancy stuff you can worry about another time.

Most companies now use some form of satellite communications, or SATCOM. This is quite simply a way to send and receive messages with the office staff at your company, most notably your dispatcher. You can type messages back and forth anytime, from anywhere. Your company will also send all of your load information to you over your SATCOM. The messages will be saved up until the point that the memory is full and then the oldest message will be deleted to make room for the newest one coming in.

Anytime someone at your company makes a promise to you or ok's something over the phone, make sure they send that message to you over the SATCOM. Your company will save all SATCOM messages for a very long time. If they sent the message to you over the SATCOM then you've basically got it in writing. You're good to go. Also, don't send any messages over the SATCOM that you wouldn't want to share with the rest of the world.

If you have to discuss something with someone and you don't want it permanently in writing, do it over the phone. Don't send a messages like, “hey, I'm out of hours and falling asleep but all I care about is money so I'm pressing on.” Can you say “prosecuting evidence”? Keep private conversations off the SATCOM.

Some of the larger companies are beginning to use radar and video cameras to help the driver increase his awareness of everything around him. As of this writing in early 2007, most of these devices help very little, and some are pretty much junk. This isn't just my opinion...this is the common opinion amongst experienced drivers. Let's talk about some of the devices you may come across.

Radar systems are an awesome idea in theory but the technology hasn't developed enough to really make it useful most of the time. One example is a unit that puts out a signal out in front of the truck and another signal along the passenger side of the tractor. The signal out the front of the truck will track your closing speed toward any obstacle in front of you. The theory is that if you are closing in on something too quickly, like a vehicle moving quite slowly in front of you, a series of lights and sounds will alert you of the danger level.

The good thing is that it works. The bad thing is that it goes off so often that after a little while you just tune it out. It sees too many obstacles and gives off too many false warnings. You may be coming up to a curve with a concrete barrier on the outside and it will see the barrier way out in front of you and warn you about it.

Well, you weren't going to hit the barrier in the first place.

It also goes off a lot when you are about to go under an overpass. I'm not talking about an overpass that's too low, just an ordinary overpass. These constant false alarms are very annoying and after a short time you just tune the unit out altogether.

The unit on the passenger side is supposed to warn you about obstacles in your blind spot. For instance if you go to change lanes from the left to the right lane on the interstate it will warn you if there is a car to your right so you don't run over top of anyone. This unit is tied into your right hand turn signal and only functions when your right hand turn signal is on.

Again though the same problem as the front unit...it sees way too many things as a threat and gives off tons of false alarms. Almost every time you put on your right hand turn signal it sees something...a bridge, a rock cliff, a concrete barrier, and sounds the alarm.

One of these two units is going off on a regular basis. It's truly annoying and I can't recall talking to any drivers that think these units are helpful. If you have these units your company will remove the ability to adjust the volume or sensitivity because they realize everyone will just shut the stupid thing off if you let em. It's not so annoying that you'll want to avoid them, but they aren't so useful that you'll want them either.

As far as video cameras go, they are starting to be mounted in mostly two places...the passenger side of the truck and the rear of the trailer. The video monitor will be placed on the dash or built into it.

The unit on the passenger side is meant to replace the mirror on the front right corner of the truck...your blind spot mirror. The theory is that you just have to glance at the screen on the dash in front of you instead of turning your head to the right to glance in your mirrors. There are a couple problems with this system. First of all, it's hard to tell what you're looking at on this small monitor compared to the reflection in a mirror. The image just isn't that clear.

Secondly, it works ok under perfect conditions, but the sun shining into the camera, rain, sleet, snow, and darkness all either limit you visibility drastically or sometimes completely render the unit useless. Again I can't recall a single driver telling me they prefer this unit to a mirror. I personally couldn't stand it.

Now the camera mounted on the rear of the trailer is great. It is intended to eliminate the rear blind spot both when driving and when backing up. Well, when you're driving, the same problems that limited the usefulness of the side-mounted camera plague this camera too. But when you're backing up the camera is great.

It lets you see exactly what's behind you and really does a great job of eliminating the blind spots, especially when backing up around a curve, which is most of the time. It also let's you see how much room is between you and an obstacle you are backing up to, like a dock or another truck at a truck stop.

Well, as you would expect from the decision-makers, the most useful of the camera and radar-based tools is the least common. My guess would be that the camera mounted on the rear of the trailer will become quite common in the coming years but as of this writing they are quite rare. Bummer.

One final tool you should have in your arsenal is a digital camera. Mainly you will use it to protect yourself. You can take pictures of the freight you're hauling, especially if something was damaged during loading or shipping, accidents, and any other events you feel you should get on film as evidence to back up your story. When something happens that could possibly be blamed on you, you don't want it to come down to your word against theirs. You want indisputable evidence.

Keep that camera close by and ready to go. Don't let yourself get in a spot where you need it quickly and its batteries are dead or you can't find it. Your window of opportunity to defend yourself may be a short one and you have to be ready when the time comes.

We've covered most of the tools at this point so let's move on to the toys. Driving truck is a whole lot more fun than it used to be. One of the main reasons is the coming of wireless and satellite-based technologies.

Wireless Internet started as a rarity, evolved into a highly useful and entertaining tool, and will soon be woven into every aspect of your life on the road. There are so many wireless 'hot spots' popping up everywhere you go that soon you will have wireless Internet coverage almost everywhere.

Already most truck stops have it available and you're finding tons of coffee shops, restaurants, bookstores, and corporations with free or nearly-free wireless Internet available. Surfing the Internet is a great way to pass the time and also a great tool to track your bank accounts, read company newsletters, and an endless variety of other things.

The Internet is an awesome way to stay in touch with family and friends. You can even set up a simple website to share pictures and stories with the world for only a few dollars a month. Email can be a great way to share pictures and stories also. Of course this is where your digital camera comes in. You can have a closeness with pictures and 'road diaries' now that you could never even come close to having before all of this technology was available.

Satellite tv and radio are nothing short of astounding. Now you have hundreds of tv and radio stations available to you anytime, from anywhere. For those of you who never traveled and tried to constantly tune in local radio and tv stations with an antennae, let me tell you how lucky you are. It was miserable.

The vast majority of the time you are out of range of any stations at all. Talk about BORING! Uh! Satellite radio and tv have made life on the road way more fun and has given you access to news and information in real time. Previously you had to count on newspapers or word of mouth. Not anymore.

You have all the news, information, and entertainment at your fingertips you could ever dream of having.

When you put it all together, in any given day you can surf the Net, communicate with your company, watch satellite tv, listen to satellite radio, share pictures and stories with the world, talk with the other drivers in the area, and generally entertain and inform the holy crap out of yourself all from the comfort of your own truck.

For those of you who never lived on the road without these luxuries let me tell you something, you'll never be able to appreciate how astounding these developments are and how much it has improved life on the road. But without a doubt you would be doing yourself a huge service to learn to use as many of these tools and toys as you can.

Driving a rig is ten times easier and more fun than it was just a few short years ago. Believe me it is!

Keep Your Head On Straight, Keep Your Act Together

Probably the most important, and most difficult to deal with, aspect of over the road driving is the mental and emotional side of it. Adapting to life on the road certainly comes easier for some than others but for everybody there will be a lot of changes. You will be spending an enormous amount of time alone and during those times you are with other people, they are always strangers...almost all the time. You're away from your home, your family, friends, and routines.

You are no longer an intimate part of the daily lives of those closest to you and there are now so many more variables and unknowns that will effect every day...weather, traffic, freight conditions, breakdowns, DOT checks, region of the country you are in, and on and on. Many people have had rather predictable days for many years...maybe most of their lives. There is nothing predictable about life on the road.

When you wake up in the morning you have almost no idea what lies ahead that day. That was one of my favorite parts of driving over the road, but that's just me. It's not nearly as enjoyable to some.

Driving truck takes a lot of patience, courage, strength, and discipline sometimes. Don't mistake me for saying it's like being in the Marines or something....let's not get crazy here...but for sure there will be times – many times – that test your character when you're on the road.

As a good example of one of those times, I'll tell you about a delivery I had to make one time. I was in Phoenix, AZ and I had a load of office furniture. It was a Friday and my delivery was scheduled for 6:00 pm delivery to city hall. I'm sent a message from dispatch telling me that they want me to call them about 30 minutes before I arrive.

So 30 minutes out I call them and they tell me the loading docks are in the basement of the city hall building and it is surrounded by one way streets. The problem is, the only way I can get backed down the ramps into the basement is to go the wrong way around the building and then get setup to back in. They were going to block the four streets off surrounding the building and I was going to come around and get backed in.

Well, it's 6:00 pm on a Friday in the dead center of downtown Phoenix. I get down there, they block off the streets, and I start coming around the building. It was the most ridiculous scene. Traffic on every single street leading to the building was at a standstill and traffic was backed up WAY down the streets. Everyone is just sitting there trying to figure out what's going on, and waiting for me. To add to the fun, the crews that are remodeling the building inside are changing shifts at the same time.

So all of the workers from both shifts – there had to be over 100 of ‘em - are lining the sidewalks next to where I'm backing in and they have nothing else to do but watch what's going on, and watch me back in. Just perfect. So the police lights are flashing on every corner, the city streets are blocked, and I have a huge audience...all at rush hour, downtown, on a Friday...watching me back in.

Luckily, I handle pressure well. It wasn't too difficult of a spot to get backed in and I got down there pretty quick and easy. I wasn't nervous, but I was keenly aware of the circumstances and a couple times I stopped for a moment to take it all in. This is just not something most people get to experience. It was amazing.

So there are times when you will be blocking traffic and causing a small scene simply because those trucks are huge and streets aren't built to a size that easy for trucks to negotiate. They build streets just big enough for trucks, so we never have much room to work with. So be prepared to just relax, be patient, and realize that you are doing an incredible service for people by transporting their goods close to where they live so that they can quickly and easily get everything they need.

If we didn't do that for them, their lives would be much more difficult...so they'll just have to wait a few minutes for you to do what you need to do sometimes. Who cares if they get impatient? It's worth it to them, whether they realize it and appreciate it or not.

It takes a lot of patience and discipline at times also. People can't stand driving behind a big, slow truck so they will be pulling out in front of you, cutting you off, and flying around you on all sides pretty much every day. You have to have the discipline and patience to deal with this stuff on a regular basis.

You can't be getting mad, tail-gating people, and getting your nerves all worked up every time another driver does something you don't like. If you do, you're going to get in accidents. Not maybe – definitely. You're also going to age an extra year for every day you're on the road!

You also have to know where and when to draw the line with people. There will be times when people will try to push you into doing things you either shouldn't be doing, or aren't comfortable with. People like your dispatcher and the shippers and receivers will try to get you to run harder than you would like or push through bad weather sometimes.

The shippers may overload you sometimes, or try loading your truck in a way that's easier for them, but either dangerous or illegally unbalanced for you. Receivers will sometimes let you sit in the parking lot for hours until they feel like unloading you or until a shift change happens so the next shift can do it instead.

You will be pushed to your limits at times and you have to be able to stand up and and say, "look, I'm responsible for this truck if something goes wrong and this is how we're going to handle this situation." You should learn to be firm when you need to, but humble and easy-going. DON'T turn every decision into a power struggle between you and them.

Relax, be calm, and work through whatever situation you are dealing with. Maybe the customers or your dispatcher won't be too pleased with the decision you've made, but believe me – if you let someone talk you into something and something goes wrong – you and you alone will be 100% responsible for it.

Everyone else will either deny talking you into it or claim ignorance to the situation at hand. No matter what, you make the final decision about handling your rig and remember that there is your career, your life, and the lives of others on the road at stake. Keep the big picture in mind and don't make a big mistake because you let yourself believe that the load you have is more important than your life and your career.

You will also be faced with a lot of time alone, away from your family and friends. I'm afraid there isn't much advice I can give you regarding how to handle this. Everyone is different when it comes to dealing with these things.

The only thing I can really say is to learn to enjoy being alone. Get into whatever interests you – reading, video games, movies...whatever. But find a way to enjoy your time alone or you're going to have a very tough time of things.

There are much better ways to stay close with people now than there ever were. Email, cell phones, and digital pictures and video can all help keep you closer with family and friends. If you're the type that shies away from technology – learn to use a laptop. It's not nearly as difficult as people make it out to be in their heads. Sharing pictures, video, and sending emails are all things that a 3rd grader can do.

Seriously.

You'll have plenty of time alone...take some of it to learn to use computers. It will quickly become a centerpiece of your daily life on the road and you won't be able to live without it ever again. Believe me.

Lastly, I think one of the most important things that helped me relax and deal with the everyday difficulties on the road was what I called having a 'shit happens' column.

Almost everything that happens can be categorized in one way or another – and sometimes there's no other way to explain something other than to say 'shit happens'. You will get traffic tickets once in a while. Your truck will break down once in a while. Your dispatcher will make a mistake or a customer won't be able to load or unload you on your scheduled day. You'll get a cold or flu once in a while. A huge snowstorm will come through right when you're on your way home. Traffic will come to a standstill because of a huge accident on the highway and you're only 5 miles from your delivery with 20 minutes to spare.

All of the things that make you say “you've GOTTA be kidding me” - they will happen every once in a while - I promise you. Keep the big picture in mind. Remember, you still have your family and friends, you still have your career, there are other drivers on the road counting on you to do your job safely, there will be other loads, and there will be better times ahead.

If you can learn to shrug things off once in a while and just realize that 'shit happens' and it's not the end of the world then you'll be much happier for sure. You can't get all distressed and totally bent out of shape every time you make a small mistake or have a bit of bad luck.

Relax, be patient, and try to roll with things. Sometimes the only other choice is to freak out, and what good does that ever do?

Shit happens...expect it and keep your cool.

In the end, I think you'll see that learning to drive a truck and learning to deal with the everyday stresses that come with driving for a living are equally important. If you can handle one well but not the other, your career will be a very short one.

Always keep the big picture in mind and anytime you consider taking a risk, ask yourself "what am I gaining vs. what am I risking by doing this?" If you look closely and consider things carefully you'll have a much better chance of avoiding problems, avoiding mistakes, and having a long, safe, enjoyable career.

In Conclusion

Well, at this point I've probably overloaded your brain with all of my stories, philosophies, and insights. You started out reading this book hoping that by the end you would know if trucking would be the right choice for you and there's a good chance that you have far more questions now than you did before.

Some lyrics from the song “Closer to Fine” by the Indigo Girls comes to mind:

“I stopped by the bar at 3 a.m.

To seek solace in a bottle or possibly a friend

And I woke up with a headache like my head against a board

Twice as cloudy as I’d been the night before

And I went in seeking clarity.”

Well, if you feel like you have more questions now than when you started reading this book then I feel like I've done my job. There are so many things to consider when it comes to making a career change – especially when the new career may be driving a truck – that you may very well never be able to come to a firm conclusion about whether or not you should go for it.

There are not many people brave enough, or in the right position in their lives, to make a firm decision without any second thoughts and just go for it. There will likely be quite a bit of uneasiness about what to do. That's a good thing.

There are a number of things you should keep in mind.

For starters, remember that this does not have to be a permanent decision. You aren't required to drive a truck for the rest of your life. I went to school to be a mechanic at one point. I paid $12,000 and the schooling took one year. I graduated, got a job, and quit after two months. I never worked for anyone as a mechanic again.

But I'm absolutely thrilled that I did it. I use the knowledge I gained from that school pretty much everyday of my life. I work on my own vehicles, my equipment for the business I now own, other people's vehicles, and there will be a million other uses for it in the future. It was worth every penny and every minute I spent at that school.

I would gladly do it again.

Secondly, keep in mind that there is no possible way to know that you are getting into a career that is right for you because truck driving is something you will have to experience in order to understand it completely. Until you've done it, there is no way to know how it will suit you. So I wouldn't necessarily shy away from doing it just because you're not certain about it.

Third, keep in mind that once you've completed the schooling and you have your license you will likely be able to go back and forth between truck driving and other jobs your entire life. There is such a huge demand for drivers that will likely continue for decades to come that trucking can be a pillar for you to fall back on whenever you need a good paying job – and quickly!

Think of the hundreds of thousands of Americans with families over the years that have lost their jobs in factories, warehouses, and elsewhere, that soon after lost their vehicles, their homes, and went bankrupt.

Think of the schooling and the CDL license as an incredible insurance policy – for a one-time fee of a few thousand dollars and a few weeks of your time you will always have a good paying job waiting for you whenever you need it. So when you look at it as an insurance policy – it makes perfect sense.

Lastly, keep in mind that you only live once and the person you are is simply the sum of your experiences. Everyday you live and everything you do should be approached as a learning experience. The more knowledge you gain throughout your life the better your life should get as time goes on. I can't promise you too many things when it comes to a career as a driver, but one thing I can promise you is that it will be a gigantic learning experience for you. Not only will you learn a new trade, but more than anything you will learn a lot about yourself.

How can you make a great life for yourself if you really don't know who you are and what's right for you, and what isn't?

You can't just hide from change and keep yourself locked away and expect to live a fulfilling life. You have to get out there and learn all you can, try as many things as possible, and then decide what's right for you. Otherwise you'll never know what you're missing.

I have always been a brave, adventurous, and independent person. I love a challenge, I love change, and I try to experience all I can in life.

I believe happiness comes from a variety of experiences that help you gain knowledge about yourself and the world around you so that you can make better and better decisions as the years go on.

If you never take a chance, never challenge yourself, and never experience any difficulties in your life, then everything you do becomes far more difficult and your decisions in day to day life are based on very little knowledge or experience, and really become more like guesses than anything else.

I really can't imagine too many scenarios where going through the schooling, getting your CDL, and trying out truck driving as a new career could be looked back upon as a mistake.

You may find that the industry and lifestyle don't suit you very well, but the experiences you'll gain and the 'insurance policy' you'll have will be more than worth the price of admission for most everyone.

In the end, there is nothing I will ever own that will be worth more to me than the memories I have of seeing the country and living on the road, the growth I've experienced as a person, and all of the adventures I've lived throughout the years I traveled – and of course all of the great people I've met.

Some of the most difficult things I've ever had to do were from behind the wheel of those trucks, but many of the best memories I will ever have include that same wheel in front of me. I can't begin to imagine who I would be and what I would be doing with my life right now if you erased everything I gained from all those years on the road.

I almost never ponder it because there is no way to know, and I'm absolutely certain I would not want to know.

For every decision you come to regret in your life you will spare yourself the agony of a hundred more in the years to come because of the knowledge you've gained.

And for every decision you make that works out well it will be followed by a hundred more that you never would have had the opportunity to make if it wasn't for that first one.

The decision to take a shot at driving a truck has turned out to be one of the very best decisions I have ever made.

The decision to take a shot a being a mechanic also turned out to be one of the very best decisions I have ever made, and I realized soon after the schooling that being a mechanic full time was not for me.

I have had people tell me they used to be a truck driver but got tired of it after a while. I've met thousands of people that did it their whole lives. But in looking back over the years, I honestly can't remember one single person telling me they regret the decision to get their CDL.

When it comes to your career, there are no guarantees in life, only opportunities. If you decide to take the opportunity to get behind the wheel, I sincerely wish you the very, very best of luck with it.

Be patient, be safe, and learn to enjoy each moment.

One thing you'll learn as a driver is to stop focusing on the destination all the time and enjoy each moment of the journey...because in the end you realize you are living the journey most of the time and the destination, in the end, is only a temporary one, and soon after a new journey begins.

This applies to life in general for all of us. Live each moment, and learn to be happy in each moment, because in the end, happiness is all that any of us is truly after. So no matter where you are and no matter what you are doing, if you are happy doing it then you've already arrived at the place you were hoping to be.

Good luck and Godspeed.

35880061R00060

Made in the USA
Lexington, KY
28 September 2014